How the Earth Works

How the Earth Works

60 Fun Activities for Exploring Volcanoes, Fossils, Earthquakes, and More

MICHELLE O'BRIEN-PALMER

CHICAGO REVIEW PRESS

Design and illustrations ©2002 by Rattray Design

©2002 by Michelle O'Brien-Palmer
All rights reserved
Published by Chicago Review Press, Incorporated
814 North Franklin Street
Chicago, Illinois 60610
ISBN 1-55652-442-0
Printed in the United States of America
5 4 3 2 1

How the Earth Works is lovingly dedicated to the two teachers who inspired me to write this book, Eileen Gibbons and Corinne Richardson. Eileen is an elementary-grade science resource teacher in Rochester, New York. Corinne teaches primary-grade students in Redmond, Washington. Both of these special teachers inspire their students through their boundless enthusiasm for science and their love of learning. It is a great honor to have worked with them.

Contents

Introduction for Parents and Teachers

How the Earth Works is all about our ever-changing Earth. It explores Earth's structure, fossils, rocks, minerals, crystals, and more. Children will learn about Earth's four layers, plate movements, and the continents. They will observe and identify fossils. Using special scientific tests, they will try to identify the mineral, rock, and crystal specimens they find as well as explore the power of volcanoes and earthquakes. Each fun activity is designed to promote learning by engaging children in a process of self-discovery using the scientific method. Children become scientists as they predict outcomes, gather materials, make scientific observations, and respond to their findings. Learning about the wonders of our dynamic planet through these hands-on activities introduces children to the process of discovery that they will use in their scientific inquiries for the rest of their lives.

The format used in the *How the Earth Works* activities is purposeful. It reflects the progression used in any scientific exploration. The basic concepts have been preserved as children are transitioned into the process of discovery using language that is familiar to them. The phrase "Did you know?" corresponds to research and new information. "You will need" introduces children to the materials needed to conduct their experiments. With the phrase "What do you think?," activities allow the child an opportunity to make an outcome prediction, or hypothesis. "Now you are ready to" explains the procedure one would follow in testing the hypothesis. The "Brain exercise" gives children an opportunity to draw conclusions from their scientific observations. Activity goals, Earth notes, keys to success, and hints are also included.

Each chapter begins with a poem that can be sung to a familiar tune. Potentially new words from the chapter are defined on the "Wonderful Words" page. The topic being explored is discussed on the page called "Dynamic Earth." An Earth Journal sheet is provided on page 3 to help children record and reflect as they connect language, art-work, and learning. Make as many copies as you need.

The "Learn More About It!" section at the end of the book references lively, fact-filled books and Internet Web sites to help you delve even further into the topics covered by the activities. The "Product and Service Information" section provides information on how to find recommended products and professionals who do workshops or assemblies related to the subject matter covered in the text.

All activities have been field-tested successfully in homes and classrooms. Most require simple materials that can be adjusted to accommodate your children. In cases where specimens may need to be purchased, alternative ways to do the activity have been suggested. For example, if fossil specimens can't be purchased, fossil information cards can be used in their place.

Initially, all of the activities will require adult supervision. After completing the activities together, many teachers and parents choose to set up learning centers using some of the activity materials on the topic being explored. This is a great way to extend and expand learning.

How the Earth Works is an exploration of the wonders of our amazing planet. Children are naturally fascinated by all aspects of Earth, from the movement of the continents to the awesome power of a volcano. Their thirst for quick facts will be quenched through fun fact or fiction cards and trivia cards. They will make their own volcanoes, mold mountains, and take a core sample from a cupcake.

This book offers science activities for many different kinds of learners. Activities reach across the curriculum, integrating language arts, music, art, mathematics, geography, history, and more into the child's exploration of Earth science. The "Chapter-by-Chapter Content and Skills Guide" on page 179 provides a quick key to the many science topics and skills touched on in each chapter.

Learning about Earth is to step back in time through the stories its fossils, minerals, rocks, and crystals tell. Take this adventure with your children. You'll never forget it!

My Earth Journal

Today I learned

How Earth Is Put Together

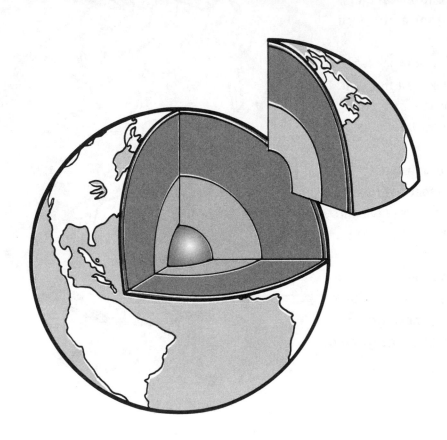

How Earth Is Put Together

Earth has four layers inside to out.
Traveling in space, it spins about.
The inner core's a solid metal ball
Known as the center of the earth to all.

The outer core is layer number two.
It's liquid iron and nickel all through.
A mantle of rock is layer three.
Crust forms the surface for land and sea.

Earth is a puzzle of 13 plates,
Slowly moving as they meet their mates.
Some collide, some slide, some let lava through
As they float beneath both me and you.

Long ago the continents were all in one.
Their constant movement is never done.
Seven continents slowly move around
On the floating plates to form the ground.

Sung to "I'm a Little Teapot"
Rocks and Shocks: Singable Science Songs, ©2001

In How Earth Is Put Together you will find

Wonderful Words from How Earth Is Put Together

Block Mountains
Block mountains are formed when pressure from deep inside Earth lifts a block of land up from between cracks (faults) in Earth's crust.

Continents
Today's continents are seven huge areas of land that slowly move on top of Earth's plates. They are Africa, Antarctica, Asia, Australia, Europe, North America, and South America.

Crust
This is the thin layer of rock that covers Earth's outer surface. Continental crust is the thickest part of Earth's crust. Oceanic crust is the thinnest part of the crust. The outer portion of Earth's crust is always changing. The bottom of the crust is very hot.

Dome Mountains
Dome mountains are formed when hot volcanic magma rises from deep inside Earth, forcing the crust into a dome shape.

Fold Mountains
Fold mountains are formed when the rock between two of Earth's plates folds upward as the plates push against each other.

Geology
Geology is the study of what Earth is made of and how its structure changes over time.

Inner Core
The inner core is a very hot solid metal ball found at Earth's center. Some scientists believe that the inner core is made of iron and nickel.

Mantle
The mantle is a very thick layer of rock found right under Earth's crust. It is made of solid rock at the top and melted rock at the bottom, where it meets Earth's outer core.

Mountains
Mountains are areas of Earth's crust that are at least two thousand feet above sea level. Mountains cover one-fourth of Earth's crust.

Outer Core
This is a layer of hot liquid iron and nickel found right beneath Earth's mantle and above the inner core.

Plates
Pieces of Earth's crust that fit together. The plates move slowly as they float on top of Earth's mantle.

Solar System
A group of nine planets, including Earth, that travel around the Sun.

Volcanic Mountains
These are cone-shaped mountains that form as magma, rocks, ash, and gases build up around an eruption.

Dynamic Earth

What should I know about Earth?

🌐 Earth is one of nine planets in our solar system. It travels through space on its journey around the Sun. The Sun is not a planet; it's a star. We can feel its heat and light on Earth.

🌐 Scientists believe that Earth was formed at least 4.5 billion years ago. It weighs approximately 13.2 septillion pounds, which equals 6.6 sextillion tons. Earth has four layers. Its center, the inner core, is a fiery hot ball of solid metal. Around the inner core is the thicker outer core, made of very hot liquid iron and nickel. The mantle is Earth's thickest layer, made of hot melted rock near the outer core and hot solid rock near Earth's crust. The crust is Earth's top, or surface, layer. Made of lighter rock, the crust is the thinnest layer of Earth.

🌐 Earth's crust is like a huge puzzle. It is divided into 13 pieces, called plates. The plates actually float on top of Earth's mantle. They move very slowly, carrying the land and ocean floor with them. The large areas of land carried by the plates are called continents. About 200 million years ago, only one continent existed. Scientists call this continent *Pangaea*, which means "all Earth." Pangaea broke apart to form the seven continents that exist today. Most of Earth is covered in water. The continents cover just over one-quarter of Earth's surface. On which continent do you live?

🌐 Mountains are made out of masses of rocks. Scientists define a mountain as land that is at least two thousand feet above sea level. About one-quarter of Earth's crust is covered in mountains. Groups of mountains are called mountain ranges. Scientists have hypothesized that some mountains, ocean floors, and valleys were formed millions of years ago as Earth cooled.

🌐 Geologists are scientists who study Earth to learn more about how it's put together and its history. They study rocks, mountains, volcanoes, and fossils to better understand our Earth.

1 Best Guess—Earth Trivia Cards

Did you know?

Scientists believe that Earth was formed at least 4.5 billion years ago.

You will need

2 sheets (8 × 11 inches) light-colored card stock
Earth Trivia Card Fronts, page 12, copied onto 1 sheet of card stock
Earth Trivia Card Backs, page 13, copied onto 1 sheet of card stock
Scissors
Glue
Partner
Rubber band

What do you think?

If I try to guess the answers for the Earth Trivia questions, I will guess ___ out of 4 correctly.

Now you are ready to

1. Cut out the 16 Earth Trivia cards from both sheets of card stock.
2. Match the question fronts to their answer backs. Glue the matching card pieces together, back-to-back. Laminate the cards if you like.
3. Place the cards with the question side up.
4. Ask your partner to give a best-guess answer to the first four questions. Once a question is answered, check the back of the card to see if it was answered correctly. How well did your partner guess?
5. Next, it is your turn to guess the answers to questions 5 through 8. How well did you guess?
6. When you are finished, wrap a rubber band around the cards to keep them together.

Activity Goal	**Earth Note**	**Key to Success**	**Hint**
To learn new information about Earth in a fun trivia card game.	Scientists estimate that Earth weighs about 6.6 sextillion tons, which is 13.2 septillion pounds.	One partner needs to be able to read. Some children may need help cutting out and gluing the cards.	Children love playing with the trivia cards. It's a fun challenge for them to test their knowledge over and over.

Earth Trivia Card Fronts

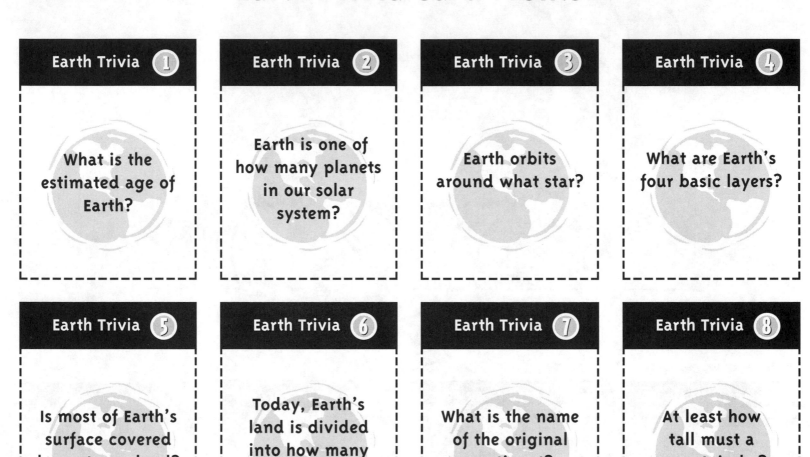

Earth Trivia ①

What is the estimated age of Earth?

Earth Trivia ②

Earth is one of how many planets in our solar system?

Earth Trivia ③

Earth orbits around what star?

Earth Trivia ④

What are Earth's four basic layers?

Earth Trivia ⑤

Is most of Earth's surface covered by water or land?

Earth Trivia ⑥

Today, Earth's land is divided into how many continents?

Earth Trivia ⑦

What is the name of the original continent?

Earth Trivia ⑧

At least how tall must a mountain be?

How the Earth Works, ©2002. Published by Chicago Review Press, Inc., 800-888-7471.

Earth Trivia Card Backs

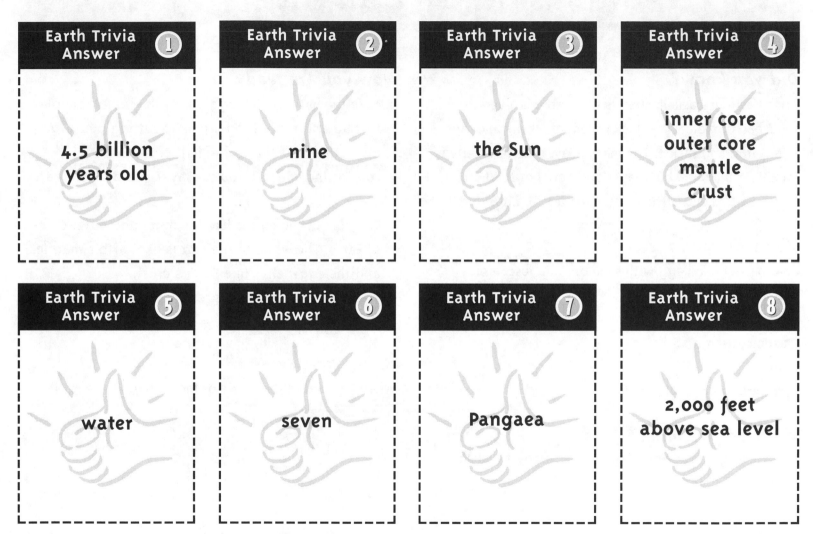

Earth Trivia Answer ①	Earth Trivia Answer ②	Earth Trivia Answer ③	Earth Trivia Answer ④
4.5 billion years old	nine	the Sun	inner core outer core mantle crust

Earth Trivia Answer ⑤	Earth Trivia Answer ⑥	Earth Trivia Answer ⑦	Earth Trivia Answer ⑧
water	seven	Pangaea	2,000 feet above sea level

How the Earth Works, ©2002. Published by Chicago Review Press, Inc., 800-888-7471.

2 Earth's Inside—Like an Egg?

Did you know?

Earth has four basic layers. Its inner core is a very hot solid ball of metal. The thick outer core is made of hot liquid iron and nickel. The mantle layer has hot melted rock near the outer core layer and very hot solid rock just below Earth's crust. The crust is made of lighter rock.

You will need

Cold hard-boiled egg with shell on, in a resealable plastic bag

Adult helper

Plastic cutting board

Knife

Refrigerator or small ice chest

What do you think?

If I look at the inside of a hard-boiled egg, it (will) or (won't) have layers.

Now you are ready to

1. Take the hard-boiled egg out of the resealable plastic bag and place it on a plastic cutting board. Ask an adult to cut the egg in half crosswise.
2. Look at the egg. Do you see layers inside? What are they?
3. The yolk of the egg is like the inner and outer cores of Earth. The white of the egg is like Earth's mantle, and the eggshell is like Earth's crust.
4. Place the egg back in its resealable bag and put it in the refrigerator.

Brain exercise

When I looked at the inside of the hard-boiled egg, it reminded me of . . .

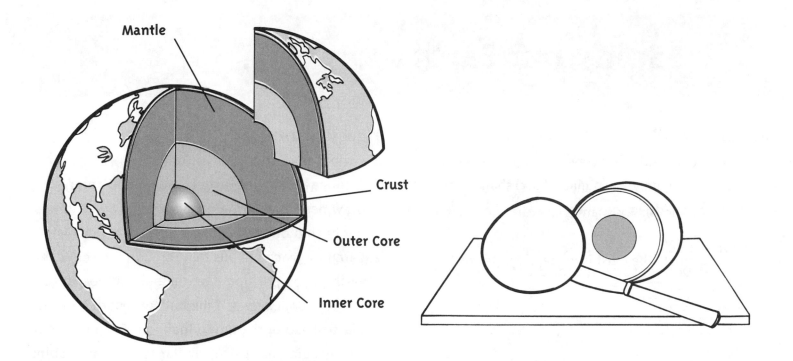

Mantle

Crust

Outer Core

Inner Core

 Activity Goal

To compare Earth's layers to a hard-boiled egg's layers.

 Earth Note

The mantle is Earth's thickest layer (approximately 1,800 miles thick), whereas Earth's crust is the thinnest layer.

 Key to Success

The egg must be cold. Try to cut it through the center, keeping the eggshell intact. The resealable bag helps to reduce the egg's odor.

 Hint

Use an apple to demonstrate Earth's layers. The center of the apple has a core, the flesh can represent the thick mantle, and the skin is thin like Earth's crust.

3 Spin Your Earth

Did you know?

Earth's inner core and outer core added together are thicker (approximately 2,200 miles thick) than the mantle and the crust added together.

You will need

Earth Spinner Design, page 17, copied onto card stock
Scissors
Crayons, markers, or colored pencils
Pushpin
Bulletin board

Now you are ready to

1. Cut out the Earth Spinner Design.
2. Color each layer of Earth in a different color.
3. Draw people, mountains, oceans, or other things you might find on Earth's crust.
4. Carefully place the pushpin through the very center of Earth as you position it on the bulletin board. Leave enough room between the bulletin board and the plastic head of the pin so that your Earth will spin.
5. Slowly spin your Earth, similar to the way it spins in space.

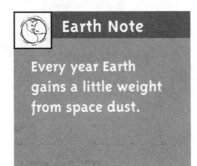 **Activity Goal**

To identify Earth's layers.

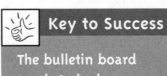 **Earth Note**

Every year Earth gains a little weight from space dust.

 Key to Success

The bulletin board needs to be low enough for the children to easily reach their Earth spinners.

Hint

Place the spinners on thin balsa wood handles as an extension to this activity.

Earth Spinner Design

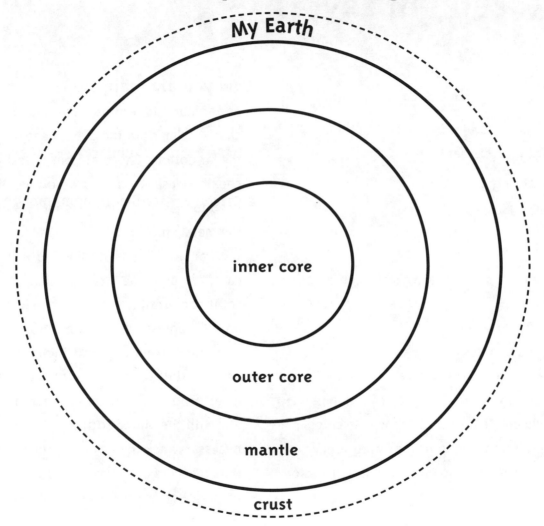

My Earth

inner core

outer core

mantle

crust

4 A Jarful of Layers

You will need

Adult helper

Microwave

Small bag of chocolate chips

16-ounce glass measuring cup

Measuring cup holding $1/8$ cup water

Metal butter knife

2 oven mitts

Clear, wide-mouthed glass jar or hard plastic container, with lid

Soap and water to wash utensils

Small bag of Red Hots candies

Small plastic container holding 5 Oreo or other cream-filled chocolate cookies whirled in a blender with a handful of mixed dark chocolate and white chocolate chips

Small piece of waxed paper cut to fit the jar bottom

Small plastic container holding 10 crushed Wheat Thins or other crackers

Now you are ready to

1. Ask an adult to use the microwave to melt enough chocolate chips in the glass measuring cup to cover the jar bottom. Chocolate burns easily, so watch the cooking closely. Add a drop or two of water if you need to make the chocolate more liquid. Stir with the metal knife.

2. With an adult's assistance and using oven mitts, carefully pour the melted chocolate into the jar. Let it cool until it is solid. The chocolate in your jar will represent Earth's inner core. Wash the glass measuring cup and the knife.

3. Ask an adult to melt enough Red Hots in the glass measuring cup to form another layer in the jar. Stir with the knife, adding a few drops of water if necessary. Ask the adult to pour the melted Red Hots over the chocolate in your jar. Can you smell the Red Hots' odor? The melted Red Hots release

their smell as an invisible gas. Let the melted Red Hots cool until solid. This represents Earth's liquid outer core.

4. Pour the crushed cookie and chocolate chip mixture into the jar. This will be your mantle layer.
5. Place the waxed paper flat inside the jar on top of the cookie layer.
6. Pour enough crushed crackers on top of the waxed paper to represent Earth's crust.
7. Place the lid on your jar. Display it in a special place where you can tell others about Earth's layers.

 Activity Goals

To measure ingredients. To observe solid, liquid, and gas states of substances. To create a model of Earth's layers.

 Earth Note

Earth's crust is very thin. It is constantly changing through weather and movement.

 Key to Success

Adult supervision and participation is absolutely necessary in this activity. Make sure you use the oven mitts when touching the glass measuring cup.

 Hint

If you add too much water, the melted candies will not solidify. Add more chocolate chips or Red Hots if this occurs. Use this activity to discuss solids, liquids, and gases.

5 Solid and Liquid—Like the Mantle

Did you know?

Earth's mantle is liquid near the hot outer core and solid near the crust.

You will need

1 tablespoon cornstarch in a small resealable plastic bag

2 teaspoons plus 2 drops of water, colored with 2 drops of red food coloring

Refrigerator

What do you think?

If I make a cornstarch mixture, it (will) or (won't) be both solid and liquid like Earth's mantle.

Now you are ready to

1. Slowly add the water to the cornstarch inside the plastic bag. Mix by sealing the bag and squeezing it. When the water and cornstarch are combined, take out the mixture and knead it with your hands. The mixture should form into a ball when you knead it and yet crumble into your hands when left alone.

2. Play with the mixture. In its solid form, it feels dry and crumbles easily. This is because it is cool.

3. As you warm up the mixture in your hands, what happens? How is this similar to what you know about Earth's mantle?

4. When you are finished, seal the bag and place it in the refrigerator.

Brain exercise

When I held the cornstarch mixture, I thought . . .

Activity Goal	Earth Note	Key to Success	Hint
To simulate the semi-solid nature of the mantle.	Like the cornstarch mixture, the mantle cracks and crumbles more easily when it is in a cooler environment.	This activity can be messy. Make sure that children are careful with the mixture. It can clog up sinks.	This mixture can only be refrigerated for short periods of time since it molds easily.

6 Core Sampling Cupcake

Did you know?

When geologists want to learn information about the inside of Earth, they take a core sample.

You will need

Hostess Cupcake or other filled cake

Small paper plate

Paper towel tube

Small garbage bag

What do you think?

If I take a core sample of a cupcake, it (will) or (won't) have layers inside.

Now you are ready to

1. Place the cupcake in the center of the paper plate. What do you predict is inside the cupcake? What clues does the outside of the cupcake give you?

2. Carefully place one end of the paper towel tube in the center of the cupcake. Hold the tube firmly as you twist it into the cupcake, pushing all the way down to the paper plate.

3. Slowly pull up on the paper towel tube. The core sample should easily fall out of the tube. If it doesn't, you may need to blow into the tube.

4. Place the outside pieces of the cupcake in the garbage bag.

5. How is the core of your cupcake similar to or different from what you predicted? Leave your cupcake core sample on display.

Brain exercise

When I looked at the core sample of the cupcake, I thought . . .

Activity Goals

To predict the inside composition of a cupcake. To compare the actual sample to the earlier prediction.

Earth Note

When geologists want to learn about Earth's structure, they drill for core samples.

Key to Success

Children enjoy having their own cupcake and sharing tubes. However, using one Hostess Cupcake in a demonstration is simple and very effective.

Hint

If working with a large group, consider making a large layered cake. Each child can use a tube end to take a core sample.

1 Slow-Floating Plates

Did you know?

Earth's crust is made of approximately 13 slow-moving plates.

You will need

Clear plastic food container with lid (a GladWare 25-ounce container works well)

Enough molasses syrup to make a $1/2$-inch layer in the bottom of the container

2 whole graham crackers

What do you think?

If broken graham crackers float on top of a layer of molasses, they (will) or (won't) collide and slide together when I move the container.

Now you are ready to

1. Carefully pour enough molasses syrup into the container to make a half-inch-deep layer in the bottom.

2. Crack the first graham cracker into two or three pieces.

3. Matching the pieces, float them on the molasses in the top half of the container. Break the second cracker into two or three pieces and place the pieces on the molasses in the lower half of the container.

4. Slowly tilt the container to one side and then to the other side. Did the graham crackers collide, glide, and slide apart as they slowly floated on top of the molasses? This is similar to how Earth's slow-moving plates float on top of the hot mantle.

5. When you are finished observing the cracker plates, place the lid on the container to prevent spilling.

6. The molasses mixture should be thrown away within 24 hours.

Brain exercise

When I looked at the cracker plates moving on the molasses mantle, I saw them . . .

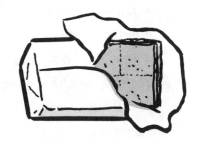

Activity Goal

To demonstrate how Earth's plates slide apart, collide, and glide over the hot mantle.

Earth Note

Colliding plates can push up mountains or create volcanoes. When plates slide past each other, earthquakes can occur. If plates separate, molten magma can rise up through the cracks.

Key to Success

The graham crackers must be placed on top of the molasses. If they are dipped into it, they might sink. In a classroom setting, only one model is needed.

Hint

Do not prepare this model ahead. After the first day, the crackers will absorb the molasses and sink. Ask children to keep the lid on the container when it is not in use.

8 Make a Model—Earth's Crust

Did you know?

The thickest part of Earth's crust is called *continental crust*. The thinner part of the crust is called *oceanic crust*.

You will need

Adult helper

1 6-ounce package strawberry Jell-O

Clear plastic food container with lid (a 14-ounce container works well)

1¼ cups boiling water in a 16-ounce glass measuring cup

Spoon

Refrigerator

¼ of any ready-made pie crust

Hard plastic table knife

Blue and green colored icing (Betty Crocker Easy Flow Decorating Icing works well)

Mug of hot water

Now you are ready to

1. Empty the Jell-O mix into the plastic food container. Ask an adult to stir in the boiling water. Continue stirring until the gelatin is completely dissolved. Refrigerate the mixture until it is firm.

2. When the gelatin is almost solid, mold a flat piece of pie crust big enough to fit over it, using the container lid as your guide.

3. Mold thinner areas for the oceanic crust and thicker areas for the continental crust.

4. Position the crust on top of the firm Jell-O. Stretch it out to cover all the gelatin. Pinch off any extra crust.

5. Once the crust is in place, use the hard plastic knife to spread green icing over the land areas. You may need to dip the knife into the hot water to make spreading easier. Finger painting the crust works well, too.

6. Rinse the knife and then spread blue icing over the ocean areas.

7. Once the icing has hardened a bit, ask an adult to help you cut one deep line horizontally through the crust (see illustration) from one side of the container to

the other. Do not cut into the gelatin. Dip the knife in the water and cut another deep horizontal line through the crust.

8. To see the plates with the hot mantle below, pull on the sides of the container and look at the red Jell-O through the two cracks.

9. Place the container at a learning center for others to view.

Brain Exercise

When I looked at the red gelatin peeking through the crust, I thought . . .

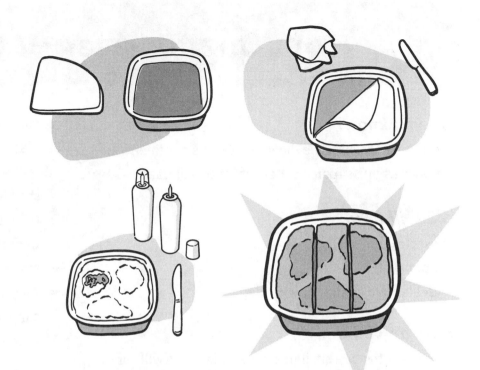

Activity Goal
To demonstrate how the plates float on top of a red-hot mantle layer.

Earth Note
Continental crust is about 25 miles thick, whereas oceanic crust is about 4 miles thick.

Key to Success
The gelatin needs to be very firm. Do not cut into the gelatin layer. Only one model is needed per home or classroom.

Hint
This activity is a huge hit. Remind your young scientists that although this model smells very tempting, scientists don't eat their models.

9 From One to Seven—Amazing Continents

Did you know?

At one time, scientists believe, all Earth's continents fit together as one supercontinent, named *Pangaea*.

You will need

2 crisp tostada shells

2 paper plates

2 resealable plastic sandwich bags

What do you think?

If I break a tostada shell into seven pieces, I (will) or (won't) be able to fit the pieces back together.

Now you are ready to

1. Carefully break one of the tostada shells into seven pieces. Place the pieces on one of the paper plates.

2. Place the whole tostada shell on the second paper plate.

3. Try to match up the pieces so that the broken tostada shell looks like the unbroken one. Can you do it?

4. Once the pieces are matched up, see how well they fit back together. Are they a perfect fit? Some fragments may have fallen off when the shell was broken.

5. Take both plates to your learning center so that others can view them. To reduce the tostada shells' odor, slip each into a resealable plastic bag.

Brain exercise

When I tried to match the seven pieces of the tostada shell, I . . .

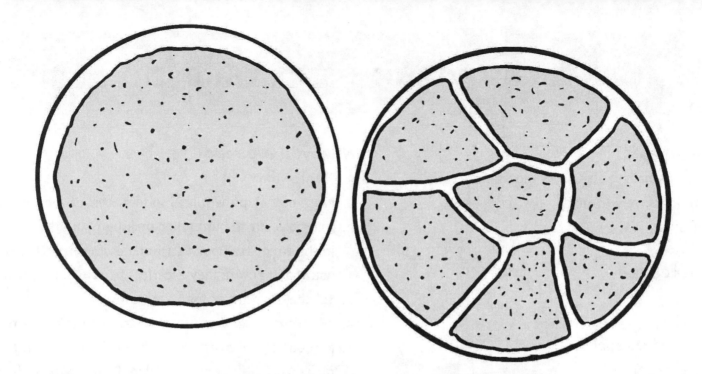

 Activity Goals

To identify similarities between Earth's plates and the tostada-shell plates. To compare broken and unbroken tostada shells.

 Earth Note

In 1912, Alfred Wegener and Frank Taylor proposed that 200 million years ago, Earth had only one supercontinent. Wegener named this first continent *Pangaea*, meaning "all Earth."

 Key to Success

The broken tostada pieces need to be large enough to fit back together somewhat easily.

 Hint

To add excitement to this activity, melt semisweet chocolate in a pie pan to make a chocolate circle that children can break and eat.

10 Baking Mountains and Valleys

Did you know?

Many scientists believe that some mountains, valleys, and ocean floors were formed millions of years ago, as Earth cooled.

You will need

Adult helper

Oven with timer

2 medium-sized red apples

1 aluminum pie pan

Oven mitts

Cooling rack

2 resealable plastic sandwich bags

What do you think?

If I compare a baked apple to a raw apple, they (will) or (won't) look the same.

Now you are ready to

1. Preheat the oven to 350° F.
2. Place one of the apples in the center of the pie pan.
3. Ask an adult to help you carefully place the pie pan in the preheated oven (use the oven mitts to protect your hands).
4. Set the oven timer for 30 minutes.
5. When the timer rings, ask an adult to take the pie pan out of the oven and place it on the cooling rack. Watch the apple as it cools down. How does it change? Reset the oven timer for 15 minutes.
6. When the timer goes off, observe the baked apple. What changes are occurring? Reset the oven timer for another 30 minutes.
7. When the timer goes off, observe the baked apple. Describe how the apple has changed.
8. Leave the baked apple out at room temperature overnight.

9. When the apple is completely cool, make observations. Does the skin remind you of valleys and mountains on Earth? Does it look different from the apple you did not bake?

10. Put the two apples in resealable plastic bags and take them to the learning center for other students to observe.

Brain exercise

When I looked at the skin of the baked apple, I thought . . .

 Activity Goals

To identify the similarities between the baked apple's skin and Earth's crust. To demonstrate how mountains and valleys might have been formed as Earth cooled.

 Earth Note

Mount Everest, the highest point of land on Earth, is located in the Himalayan mountain range.

 Key to Success

Baking makes the apple very sticky. Be sure to cook the apple at least 30 minutes to achieve the desired effect.

 Hint

The type of apple and its storage history will affect the baking time necessary. Red apples work very well when baked 30 minutes.

11 Fold-a-Mountain

Did you know?

There are four main types of mountains: fold, volcanic, block, and dome. Land must be at least 2,000 feet above sea level to be considered a mountain.

You will need

3 hand towels of different solid colors, folded into narrow lengths
Partner
Table

What do you think?

If my partner and I push the towel ends together, I (will) or (won't) be able to see how they fold into a mountain shape.

Now you are ready to

1. Place the hand towels on top of each other on the table.
2. Now you and your partner should each take one end of the towels.
3. Slowly push the towel ends toward the middle.
4. As the towels start to fold, they form a fold mountain shape. Layers of rocks pushed together can form fold mountains.
5. Place the towels flat at a learning center so others can try folding a mountain, too.

Brain exercise

When we pushed the towels' ends together, they became . . .

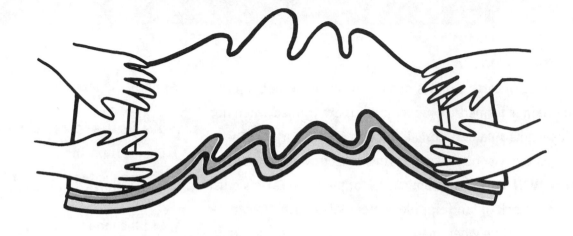

 Activity Goal

To demonstrate how fold mountains are formed when layers of rocks are pushed together.

 Earth Note

When Earth's plates move together, mountains can be formed. Groups of mountains are called *mountain chains* or *mountain ranges*.

 Key to Success

Different solid colors of towels are needed to demonstrate the layering effect.

 Hint

Model this activity for the children first. If hand towels are not available, substitute paper towels for the hand towels. Dampen the paper towels to make them more pliable.

12 Fold, Dome, Block, and Volcano

Did you know?

When two of Earth's plates push against each other, a fold mountain is formed. Dome mountains are formed when hot volcanic magma can't break through Earth's surface. The magma pushes the rocks of Earth's crust upward into a dome shape. When pressure from cracks, or faults, in Earth's crust heave a block of land up, block mountains form. Volcanic mountains form when magma, rocks, gases, and ash gradually build up in a cone shape around an eruption.

You will need

Partner

Mountain illustrations, page 36, copied onto card stock and cut out (laminate if you like)

Crayola clay in at least 3 earth tones

Clean work surface

Construction paper for base of clay mountain (black works well)

Pencil

White sticky label

Now you are ready to

1. Choose a partner.
2. Choose the type of mountain you and your partner would like to mold.
3. Use the mountain illustrations as a model for your mountain. Select the clay colors you want to use in molding your mountain. What are the special features of your mountain?
4. Take your clay and start molding your mountain on a clean work surface. When finished, place it on the construction paper base.
5. Write your mountain's name on a sticky label. Place the label on your base.
6. Learn as much as you can about your mountain. Share the mountain model with your friends.
7. If you are in a classroom, look at your classmates' mountains. Ask questions to learn more about them.

 Activity Goals

To identify the features of one type of mountain. To construct one of the four types of mountains.

 Earth Note

The Appalachian mountains are fold mountains. The Black Hills are dome mountains. The Sierra Nevada mountains are block mountains, and the Cascade mountains are volcanic mountains.

 Key to Success

Stimulate creativity by making several colors of clay available to the children. Table groups working in pairs but on the same mountain type work well.

 Hint

If Crayola clay is not available, Plasticine works fine. The clay needs to be pliable enough to manipulate easily.

Kinds of Mountains

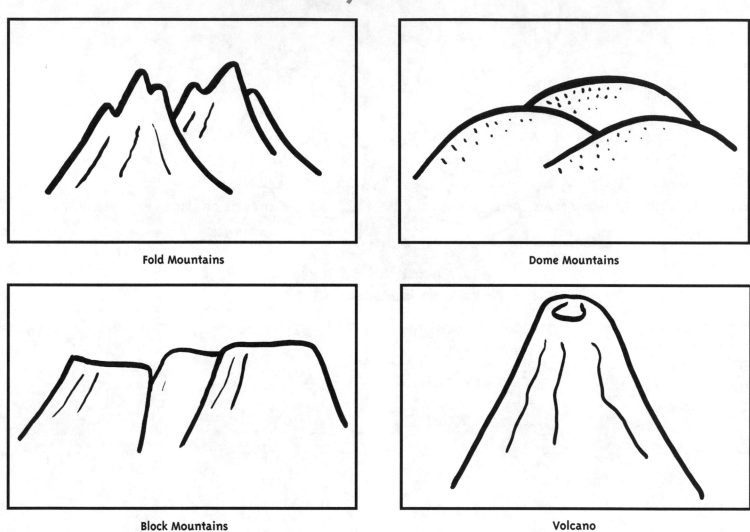

Fold Mountains

Dome Mountains

Block Mountains

Volcano

How the Earth Works, ©2002. Published by Chicago Review Press, Inc., 800-888-7471.

13 Match Up—What's That Continent?

Did you know?

Earth's seven continents are Africa, Antarctica, Asia, Australia, Europe, North America, and South America.

You will need

What's That Continent? Bingo Board, page 38, copied onto card stock

What's That Continent? Name Cards, page 39, copied onto card stock

Laminating materials (optional)

Scissors

Answers, page 180

Now you are ready to

1. Cut out all the name cards.
2. Look at your What's That Continent? Bingo Board. Find the name card that you think goes with each picture on the board.
3. Check the answers on page 180 to see how many continents you matched correctly.
4. Did you make a bingo?
5. Try making a bingo again later and see how much you've learned.

 Activity Goal

To identify the seven continents and Pangaea.

 Earth Note

Continents usually include the nearby islands.

 Key to Success

Refer to the globe, pointing out the continents, before children play this game.

 Hint

Children love testing their knowledge.

What's That Continent? Bingo Board

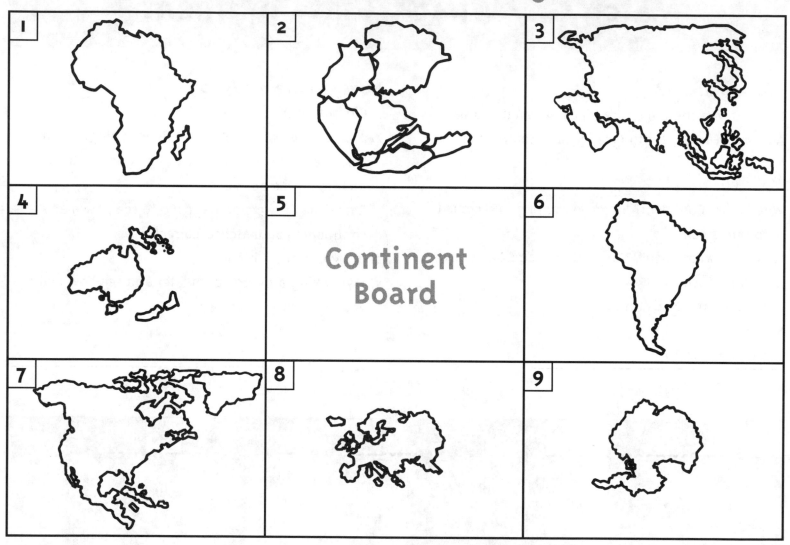

1	2	3
4	5 Continent Board	6
7	8	9

What's That Continent? Name Cards

Antarctica

Asia

North America

Europe

South America

Pangaea

Australia

Africa

Fantastic Fossils

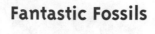

Fantastic Fossils

She'll be digging for a fossil someday soon.
He'll be sifting through the sand on a sand dune.
She'll be reaching for a bone. He'll be searching for unknowns.
She'll be checking rocks and stones, someday soon.

Fossils must be at least 10,000 years old!
What amazing tales of ancient Earth they hold.
They may come from land or sea, telling us Earth's history,
Unlocking ancient stories that have gone untold.

They're remains of ancient plants and animals, too.
Fos-sil-i-za-tion takes millions of years to do.
There are fossil casts and molds. There are shark teeth to behold.
Mammoths trapped in glacial cold are fossils, too.

She'll be digging for a fossil someday soon.
He'll be sifting through the sand on a sand dune.
She'll be reaching for a bone. He'll be searching for unknowns.
She'll be checking rocks and stones, someday soon.

Sung to "She'll Be Coming 'Round the Mountain"
Rocks and Shocks: Singable Science Songs, ©2001

In Fantastic Fossils you will find

Wonderful Words from Fantastic Fossils

Amber
Amber is the fossilized sap of an ancient plant. The sticky sap trapped insects, frogs, spiders, and other creatures and then hardened around them, preserving them for millions of years.

Ammonite Fossil
This is an extinct sea creature with a shell like a snail's. The ammonite's closest relative today is the nautilus.

Belemnite Fossil
This extinct sea creature had a pointed, cigar-shaped inside shell, similar to today's squid.

Cast Fossil
When minerals and rock materials replace the remains of an ancient animal or plant, a cast fossil is formed.

Extinct
Plants and animals that no longer live on Earth are extinct.

Fossil Fuels
These fuels are produced from the remains of ancient plants and animals. Coal and oil are fossil fuels.

Fossils
Fossils are the remains or tracings of plants and animals preserved in mud, peat, sand, or other materials for at least 10,000 years.

Limestone
Limestone is a sedimentary rock made up mainly of the mineral calcite. Fossils are found in limestone more often than in any other rock.

Mold Fossil
The shape or imprint that the remains of an ancient plant or animal has left in a rock is called a *mold fossil*.

mya
This abbreviation stands for **m**illion **y**ears **a**go.

Paleontologist
A paleontologist is a scientist who studies fossils.

Remains
Remains are what is left after a plant or animal decays. Remains are usually hard body parts, such as seeds, woody stems, bones, and shells.

Sedimentary Rock
When layers of mud, ground-up rock, clay, and sometimes fossils of plants or shells harden or cement together, they become sedimentary rock. Fossils are most commonly found in sedimentary rock.

Sediments
Sediments are layers of mud, clay, and ground-up grains of rock that collect on the bottom of rivers, lakes, or oceans.

Shale
Shale is a sedimentary rock made mostly of clay. Fossils are often found in shale.

Trace Fossils
Trace fossils preserve the movements and activities of animals. Tracks, trails, and burrows are trace fossils.

Trilobite Fossil
This extinct sea animal had a segmented body and jointed legs like today's crab.

Zone Fossils
These fossils appear in only one geologic period or era. Zone fossils are used to tell the age of the rocks in which they are found.

Dynamic Earth

What should I know about fossils?

🌏 The word *fossil* means "dug up." Paleontology is the study of fossils. Fossils are the remains of plants and animals preserved in mud, peat, sand, rock, and other materials. Fossilization takes place over thousands or millions of years. To be called fossils, preserved plants and animals must be at least 10,000 years old.

🌏 Teeth, bones, claws, shells, and scales of ancient animals are the most commonly found fossils. Leaves, stems, and the wood of ancient plants can also become fossils. Scientists study fossils to learn more about the history of life on Earth.

🌏 Most fossils are found in sedimentary rocks such as limestone or shale. It is more common to find fossils of ocean-dwelling creatures than land-dwelling creatures. Animals and plants from the land are usually found in the mud and sand of a lake or river bottom. Animals and plants are sometimes found preserved in ice, tar, peat, and a hardened saplike substance called amber.

🌏 A mold fossil is formed when the shape of an ancient plant or animal forms a hollow in a rock. If a mold fossil fills with new material, a cast fossil forms. A trace fossil forms when the trail of an animal's activities is preserved through fossilization.

🌏 Coal and oil are fossil fuels. They come from the remains of ancient plants and animals. Fossil fuels provide energy and are used to make many materials we buy today. The polyester in your clothing, your plastic sunglasses, and the crayons you use to draw with are all by-products of the oil that comes from fossils.

🌏 Paleontology is a very important science. Fossils help us learn more about the plants and animals that lived on Earth before us.

1 Fossil Fact or Fiction

Did you know?

At one time, long ago, anything "dug up" was called a fossil. Today, only ancient plants and animals over 10,000 years old are identified as fossils.

You will need

2 sheets (8½ × 11 inches) light-colored card stock

Fossil Fact or Fiction Card Fronts, page 48, copied onto 1 sheet of card stock

Fossil Fact or Fiction Card Backs, page 49, copied onto 1 sheet of card stock

Scissors

Glue

Partner

Rubber band

What do you think?

If I try to guess the answers for Fossil Fact or Fiction, I will guess __ out of 4 correctly.

Now you are ready to

1. Cut out the 16 Fossil Fact or Fiction cards from both sheets of card stock.
2. Match the card fronts to their answer backs. Glue the matching card pieces together, back-to-back. Laminate the cards if you like.
3. Place the cards with the answer side down.
4. Ask your partner to guess fact or fiction for the first four cards, making his or her best guess. Each time your partner answers, check the back of the card to see if he or she was right. How well did your partner guess?
5. Next it is your turn to guess fact or fiction for the last four cards, making your best guess. How well did you guess?
6. When you are finished, wrap a rubber band around the cards to keep them together.

Activity Goal	Earth Note	Key to Success	Hint
To learn new information about fossils in a fun fact or fiction card game.	Paleontologists believe, from their study of fossils, that life originated on Earth at least 3,500 million years ago (mya).	One partner needs to be able to read. Some children may need help cutting out and gluing the cards.	Children love playing with the fact or fiction cards. These cards are a great way for children to learn new information and test their knowledge.

Fossil Fact or Fiction Card Fronts

Fantastic Fossils Fact or Fiction ① Paleontologists only study dinosaurs.	**Fantastic Fossils Fact or Fiction** ② Fossils are the remains of plants or animals.

Fantastic Fossils Fact or Fiction ③ The land produces more fossils than the ocean.	**Fantastic Fossils Fact or Fiction** ④ Most fossils are shells, teeth, wood, or bones.

Fantastic Fossils Fact or Fiction ⑤ Fossils must be at least 40 years old.	**Fantastic Fossils Fact or Fiction** ⑥ Ancient insects preserved in amber for millions of years are fossils.

Fantastic Fossils Fact or Fiction ⑦ Coal and oil are fossil fuels.	**Fantastic Fossils Fact or Fiction** ⑧ Burning fossil fuels can cause air pollution.

Fossil Fact or Fiction Card Backs

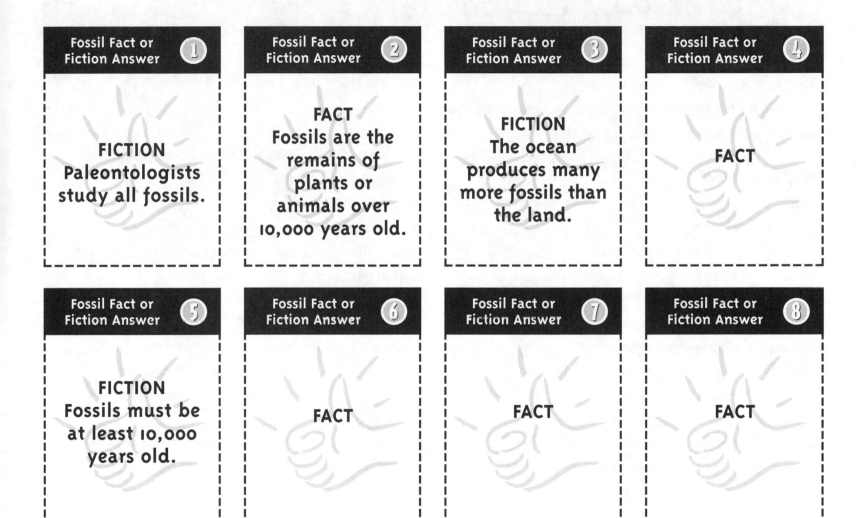

Fossil Fact or Fiction Answer ①

FICTION
Paleontologists study all fossils.

Fossil Fact or Fiction Answer ②

FACT
Fossils are the remains of plants or animals over 10,000 years old.

Fossil Fact or Fiction Answer ③

FICTION
The ocean produces many more fossils than the land.

Fossil Fact or Fiction Answer ④

FACT

Fossil Fact or Fiction Answer ⑤

FICTION
Fossils must be at least 10,000 years old.

Fossil Fact or Fiction Answer ⑥

FACT

Fossil Fact or Fiction Answer ⑦

FACT

Fossil Fact or Fiction Answer ⑧

FACT

How the Earth Works, ©2002. Published by Chicago Review Press, Inc., 800-888-7471.

2 Fossil Collection Starter

Did you know?

You can buy fossils from rock and gem stores around the country. See Product Information, page 181.

You will need

Adult helper

Specimen 1, ammonite

Specimen 2, small belemnite

Specimen 3, small trilobite

Specimen 4, small ancient shark tooth

Specimen 5, small fossilized snail

Specimen 6, dinosaur bone fragment

Specimen 7, dinosaur eggshell fragment

Specimen 8, small piece of amber

Fine-point correction pen (white ink)

Fine-point permanent pen (black ink)

3 sheets (8½ x 11 inches) light-colored card stock

Fossil Information Cards (pages 52 and 53) copied onto the card stock

Scissors

Glue

Magnifying glass or jeweler's loupe (see Product Information, page 181)

Rubber band

Plastic lidded case with dividers (see Product Information, page 181) or large empty egg carton with cotton padding

Now you are ready to

1. With an adult's help, make a very small white circle on each fossil, using the correction pen. These circles will be used to number the fossils. Let the circles dry.

2. Ask an adult to use the permanent pen to write each specimen's number (listed above) in its white circle.

3. Cut out the information cards from the sheets of card stock. Match the information card fronts to their backs. Glue the matching cards together. Laminate the cards if you like.

4. Use the magnifying glass to study each fossil.

5. Read the information cards to learn more about each fossil.

6. When you are finished with this activity, put your fossil specimens in your fossil case. Wrap a rubber band around the information cards to keep them together. Store the cards with your fossil case.

 Activity Goals

To collect and store fossils. To identify a number of fossils.

 Earth Note

Fossils can be millions of years old. They need to be handled carefully and treated with great respect.

 Key to Success

The white circles for the numbers should be very small and unobtrusive. Place the fossil case at a learning center where children can explore each fossil.

 Hint

If you are unable to purchase the fossils, go to your nearest natural history museum to view their fossils.

Fossil Information Card Fronts

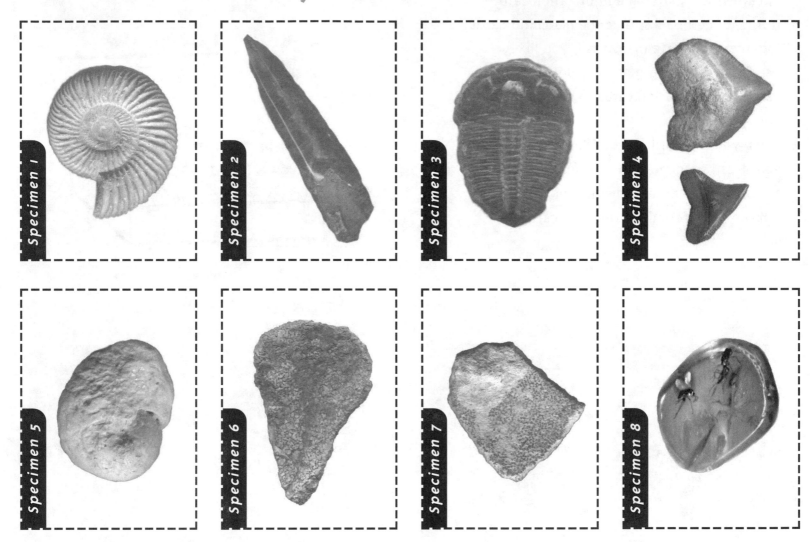

Specimen 1

Specimen 2

Specimen 3

Specimen 4

Specimen 5

Specimen 6

Specimen 7

Specimen 8

How the Earth Works, ©2002. Published by Chicago Review Press, Inc., 800-888-7471.

Fossil Information Card Backs

Fossil Information Card 1
ammonite
This is the fossil of an extinct sea animal. It had an outside shell similar to a snail shell. Today's nautilus is related to the ammonite.

Fossil Information Card 2
belemnite
This is the fossil of an extinct sea animal with a cigar-shaped inside shell similar to today's squid.

Fossil Information Card 3
trilobite
This is the fossil of an extinct sea animal. It had a segmented body and jointed legs like a crab.

Fossil Information Card 4
shark tooth
This is the tooth of an ancient shark. Sharks have lived from 135 mya through today.

Fossil Information Card 5
fossilized snail
This is a fossil of a snail. Snails have a coiled outside shell.

Fossil Information Card 6
dinosaur bone fragment
This is a small piece of a fossilized dinosaur bone. Dinosaurs were reptiles.

Fossil Information Card 7
dinosaur eggshell fragment
Dinosaurs laid eggs, since they were reptiles. This is small piece of a dinosaur eggshell.

Fossil Information Card 8
amber
This is the fossilized sap of an ancient plant. Sticky amber trapped insects, frogs, spiders, and other creatures.

How the Earth Works, ©2002. Published by Chicago Review Press, Inc., 800-888-7471.

3 Folding Up—Fossils Uncovered

Did you know?

Many fossils are uncovered when Earth's plates move.

You will need

Adult helper

Pencil

Ruled index card

4 different colors of clay, each rolled out into a flat rectangle (5 × 3 inches) about $1/2$ inch thick

Flat work surface covered with waxed paper

Can or box of sea salt

Table knife

What do you think?

If I make a fold mountain and cut off its top, it (will) or (won't) show me one way that fossils can be uncovered.

Now you are ready to

1. Write the number 4 on the first line of your index card. Write the number 3 on the next line. Do the same on the next line for the number 2, and then write the number 1 on the next line.

2. Place the first clay rectangle on the waxed paper. Shake the sea salt over the clay. The first clay rectangle will represent the oldest layer of rock. The sea salt on top of it will represent the oldest fossils. Write the color of clay for the oldest layer next to the number 1 on your index card.

3. Fit the second clay rectangle on top of layer 1. Shake your imaginary sea salt fossils on top of it. Write the color of the second clay rectangle next to the number 2 on your index card.

4. Repeat step 3 with the third and fourth layers.

5. Push both ends of your layered clay toward each other to make a fold mountain shape.

6. Ask an adult to slice off the top of the mountain with the table knife.

7. Look at the mountain now. Do you see any sea salt fossils? What colored layers are showing? Where is the oldest layer (color number 1)? Do its fossils show? Can you see why fold mountains uncover old fossils?

Brain exercise

When I saw the top of the fold mountain, I thought . . .

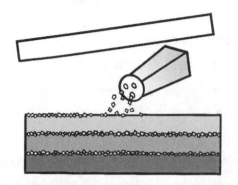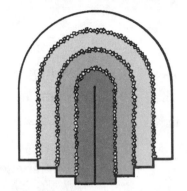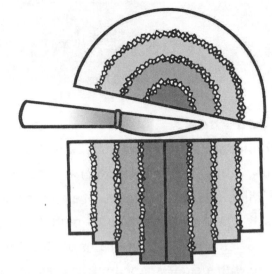

Activity Goal	**Earth Note**	**Key to Success**	**Hint**
To demonstrate one way that Earth's movements uncover fossils.	When a fold mountain forms, the oldest rock layer ends up at the top center of the mountain. The youngest rock layer forms the mountain's sides. Weathering by ice and wind removes the mountain's top and exposes its fossils.	It is important to use different colors of clay to clearly define the rock layers.	Prepare the clay rectangles ahead of time. To make the age of the fossils even clearer, use food coloring on the sea salt.

4 Fossil Find

Did you know?

Ammonites are the remains of an extinct squidlike sea creature with an outside shell similar to today's snail shell. Trilobites are the remains of an extinct sea creature with a segmented body and jointed legs like a crab's. Belemnites are the remains of an extinct sea creature with a cigar-shaped inside shell similar to today's squid.

You will need

Large piece of newspaper

Plastic container with lid, filled with sand (a short, round 14-ounce container works well)

Partner

3 very small seashells

Specimens from Fossil Collection Starter, activity #2, page 50

> Specimen 1, ammonite
>
> Specimen 2, belemnite
>
> Specimen 3, trilobite

Fossil information cards for each of the listed fossils

2 small plastic paintbrushes, 1 with finer and 1 with thicker bristles

Fossil case

What do you think?

If fossils are hidden in the sand, I (will) or (won't) be able to find them and correctly identify them.

Now you are ready to

1. Place newspaper underneath the container. Ask your partner to hide the small shells and the fossils in the sand.
2. Before you begin your search, look at the fossil information cards. Try to pronounce the names of the fossils.
3. Can you see anything other than sand? Slowly and carefully, lightly dust the surface of the sand with one of the paintbrushes. Do you see anything more now? When a fossil or shell is uncovered, carefully place it on the newspaper.

4. Test both types of brushes to see which one you prefer as a fossil-cleaning tool.

5. Did you find a fossil or a shell? If you think it's a fossil, check your fossil information card. Does the white circle on the fossil match the number on the card? What type of fossil is it? Read the back of the fossil information card to learn more.

6. Repeat steps 3 through 5 until you have found all of the fossils and shells hidden in the sand.

7. Now it's your turn to hide the fossils and shells for your partner. Start over with steps 2 through 6.

8. When you are finished, place the cleaned fossils and the fossil information cards back inside the fossil case.

Brain Exercise

When I used the smaller brush, I . . .

Activity Goals	Earth Note	Key to Success	Hint
To demonstrate uncovering fossils. To test and evaluate different brushes. To examine and identify three fossils.	Ammonites are zone fossils. They help date rocks found in the Jurassic period.	This is a great partner activity. The container of sand is too small for more than two children at a time. It can get messy.	Once children learn about other fossils, they enjoy hiding them in the sand as well.

5 Take a Closer Look I—Shark Sharp

Did you know?

Sharks have existed for millions of years. Shark teeth are common fossils. Like today's sharks, ancient sharks grew new teeth to replace the teeth that fell out. Scientists think that the extinct Carcharodon, an ancient relative to today's shark, had a body length of over 39 feet.

You will need

Specimen 4, ancient shark tooth, from Fossil Collection Starter, activity #2, page 50

Magnifying glass or jeweler's loupe (see Product Information, page 181)

Fossil information card for shark tooth

Pencil

Paper

Fossil case

What do you think?

If I look at an ancient shark tooth, it (will) or (won't) have sharp edges.

Now you are ready to

1. Use the magnifying glass to take a closer look at the ancient shark tooth. Carefully touch and turn the shark tooth around. What color is it? What shape is it? Is it hard or soft? Does it look sharp? Why might ancient sharks have needed sharp teeth?
2. Read about the shark tooth on the information card.
3. Record your observations in writing and in drawings with your pencil and paper.
4. When you are finished looking at the shark tooth, place it and the information card back in your fossil case.

Brain exercise

When I looked at the ancient shark tooth, I thought . . .

ancient shark teeth

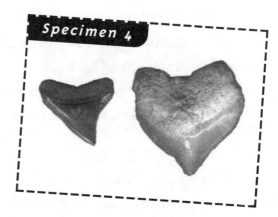

Specimen 4

Activity Goal

To examine an ancient shark tooth.

Earth Note

Creatures that lived on the ocean floor are among the most common fossils. Most of these creatures had hard shells or other parts that fossilized well.

Key to Success

Children should handle the shark tooth carefully. Nonreading children will need a partner who can read the card to them.

Hint

Many children own shark teeth. They enjoy comparing the ancient shark tooth to a present-day shark tooth.

Did you know?

Some present-day snails are very colorful. Most fossil snails have lost their original color. They may have been colorful, too.

You will need

Magnifying glass or jeweler's loupe (see Product Information, page 181)

Snail shell from outdoors

Specimen 5, fossilized snail, from Fossil Collection Starter, activity #2, page 50

Fossil information card for fossil snail

Pencil

Paper

Fossil case

What do you think?

If I look at a present-day snail, it (will) or (won't) be shaped like a snail that lived more than 10,000 years ago.

Now you are ready to

1. Use the magnifying glass to take a closer look at the present-day snail shell. Carefully touch and turn the shell around. What color is it? What shape is it? Is it hard or soft?

2. Look at the fossil snail with the magnifying glass. What color is it? What shape is it? Is it hard or soft? How is it similar to the other snail shell? How is it different?

3. Read about the fossil snail on the information card.

4. Record your observations in writing and in drawings with your pencil and paper. You may want to include a drawing of a present-day snail shell if you have room.

5. When you are finished looking at the fossil snail, place it and the information card back in your fossil case.

Brain exercise

When I looked at the fossilized snail shell, I thought . . .

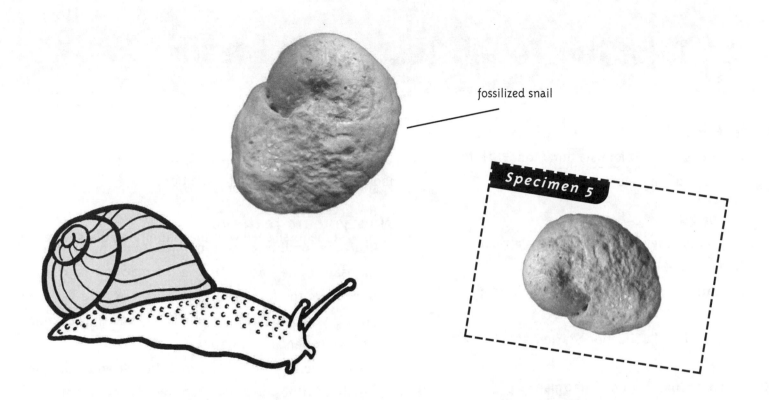

fossilized snail

Specimen 5

 Activity Goal

To examine a fossil snail and compare it to a present-day snail.

 Earth Note

Snails are often found as fossils because their hard shells do not decay.

 Key to Success

Find a snail shell from outdoors before the activity begins. Nonreading children will need a reading partner.

 Hint

If you can't find a snail shell outside, substitute a picture of a present-day snail from an encyclopedia.

7 Take the Touch Test—Dino Fossils

Did you know?

Dinosaurs were reptiles. Scientists think today's birds might be related to dinosaurs.

You will need

Magnifying glass or jeweler's loupe (see Product Information, page 181)

Fossil information cards for dinosaur bone and eggshell fragments

Specimens from Fossil Collection Starter, activity #2, page 50

    Specimen 6, dinosaur bone fragment

    Specimen 7, dinosaur eggshell fragment

Pencil

Paper

Dried chicken bone in a resealable plastic bag

Chicken eggshell fragment (from a hard-boiled egg only)

Fossil case

What do you think?

If I look at a dinosaur bone fragment, it (will) or (won't) look like a present-day chicken bone.

Now you are ready to

1. Read the fossil information card about the fossilized dinosaur bone fragment. Use the magnifying glass to observe the fossilized dinosaur bone fragment. Record your observations in writing and in drawings with your pencil and paper.

2. Look at the dried chicken bone. Does it look like the fossilized dinosaur bone fragment? How is it similar? How is it different?

3. Read the fossil information card about the fossilized dinosaur eggshell fragment. Use the magnifying glass to observe the fossilized dinosaur eggshell fragment. Draw your observations.

4. Look at the chicken eggshell fragment. Does it look like the fossilized piece of dinosaur eggshell? How is it similar? How is it different?
5. When you are finished looking at the fossilized dinosaur bone and eggshell fragments, place them and the information cards back in your fossil case.

dinosaur bone fragment

dinosaur eggshell fragment

Brain exercise

When I compared the fossilized dinosaur bone fragment to the present-day dried chicken bone, I thought . . .

Activity Goals	Earth Note	Key to Success	Hint
To compare a fossilized bone to a present-day bone. To observe how minerals have replaced the original bone.	Fossilization has replaced the dinosaur bone with minerals and rock materials. Fossilization takes place over thousands or millions of years.	The chicken eggshell must come from a hard-boiled egg. The chicken bone must be completely dry. If possible, it should be kept inside a resealable plastic bag at all times.	If you can't find a dinosaur bone or eggshell fragment, try substituting petrified wood and comparing it to present-day wood.

8 Fossilized Insects—Set in Soap

Did you know?

Sticky amber trapped insects, frogs, spiders, and other creatures, preserving them for millions of years.

You will need

Adult helper

Magnifying glass or jeweler's loupe (see Product Information, page 181)

Specimen 8, amber, from Fossil Collection Starter, activity #2, page 50

Pencil

Paper

Petroleum jelly

1 plastic ice cube tray

8 dead insects or 8 plastic insects

1 bar amber-colored glycerin soap (found in grocery and drug stores), unwrapped

1 16-ounce glass measuring cup with pour spout

Microwave

Oven mitt

Fossil information card for amber

Fossil case

Resealable bag

Red and orange food coloring to dye soap if amber-colored soap is unavailable.

Now you are ready to

1. Read the fossil information card about amber. Use the magnifying glass to observe the fossilized amber. Record your observations in writing and in drawings with your pencil and paper.
2. Lightly cover the sides and bottom of eight individual ice cube molds with petroleum jelly. Place one insect in each mold.

3. Drop the unwrapped amber-colored glycerin soap into the measuring cup.

4. Place the measuring cup in the microwave. Heat the soap until fully melted. The timing varies with individual microwaves.

5. With an adult's help, use the oven mitt to pour the melted soap into each mold, forming a small piece of amber soap. For larger amber pieces, use two bars of soap per ice cube tray.

6. When the soap has solidified (20 to 30 minutes), pop it out of the tray.

7. Use the magnifying glass to take a closer look at your amber soap with the insect inside. How is it similar to fossilized amber? How is it different from fossilized amber?

8. When you are finished comparing the fossilized amber to the amber soap, place the real amber and the information card back in your fossil case. Place your soap amber inside a resealable plastic bag for future viewing.

Brain exercise

When I looked at the amber soap, I thought . . .

 Activity Goal

To simulate trapping an insect in sticky amber.

 Earth Note

Amber preserves insects in their natural state. This makes them easier to study than fossil molds and casts.

 Key to Success

Dead insects are plentiful in most homes and schools. Make sure you have enough soap to make a cube for every child. Consider making one sample cube with a real insect and the rest with plastic insects.

 Hint

If insects are floating on top of the soap mixture, pour two layers of soap into the mold. Let the first layer solidify and then pour a second thin layer over the insect.

Did you know?

Mammoths, ancient elephant-like creatures, were pre-served in the frozen ground of Siberia. Scientists estimate that the largest type of mammoth grew to 13 feet tall.

You will need

1 shell

1 fresh cherry or berry

1 dead insect

Magnifying glass or jeweler's loupe (see Product Information, page 181)

1 plastic ice cube tray

Water

Refrigerator with freezer

Paper towels

Now you are ready to

1. Observe the shell, cherry, and insect with the magnifying glass. Place each item inside its own mold in the ice cube tray.
2. Fill the molds half full of water.
3. Place the tray in the freezer section of the refrigerator.
4. After 30 minutes, pull the tray out. Has the water frozen? Has it turned from liquid water to solid ice yet?
5. Add more water until the molds are almost full. Place the tray back in the freezer until the water is frozen solid.
6. When the ice cubes are solid, pop them out of the mold. Hold them with a paper towel. Can you see the shell, the cherry, and the insect? How do they look?
7. Use the magnifying glass to take a closer look. Have any of the frozen objects changed?

Brain exercise

When I observed the frozen cherry, it was . . .

Activity Goals	Earth Note	Key to Success	Hint
To observe liquid changing to solid. To examine frozen specimens. To observe and discuss visual changes.	Earth has had a number of ice ages. Ancient animals preserved in ice are usually very well preserved.	Keep paper towels available. This activity can get a bit wet as the ice melts.	Try freezing a grape to see how well ice preserves it.

10 Mold and Cast Fossils

Did you know?

A mold fossil is the indentation or impression left in rock by the remains of an ancient plant or animal. If mineral and rock materials fill the indentation, a cast fossil is formed.

You will need

Newspaper

Flat working surface

Golf-ball-sized piece of Crayola clay or similar clay

Petroleum jelly

Cotton swab

Small shell

Plaster of paris

Plastic cup

Water

Hard plastic table knife

Now you are ready to

1. Cover the working surface with newspaper.

2. Roll the clay into a ball.

3. Dip the cotton swab into petroleum jelly. Coat the outside of the shell with the jelly.

4. Press the outer surface of the shell into the clay hard enough to make an indentation. Carefully pull the shell out of the clay. Look where the shell used to be. You have just made a mold of the shell. This is like a mold fossil.

5. Make a small portion of plaster of paris paste in the plastic cup. Try using 2 tablespoons of plaster of paris to 1 tablespoon of water for one shell. Pour the water in first and then pour the plaster of paris into the water. Let it sit for 2 minutes (do not stir).

6. Now stir the plaster of paris with the hard plastic knife. The mixture should be somewhat thick.

7. Fill the clay mold completely with the paste. Use the knife to level the paste inside the mold.

Step #3

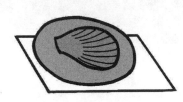

Step #4a

Step #4b
Mold Fossil

Step #7

8. Let the paste harden in the mold overnight. In the morning, pop the cast out of the clay. Your cast is like a cast fossil. A real cast fossil fills with minerals and rock materials. Your cast hardened overnight, but a real cast fossil takes thousands or millions of years to fossilize.

9. Compare the original shell to the shell cast. How are they similar? How are they different?

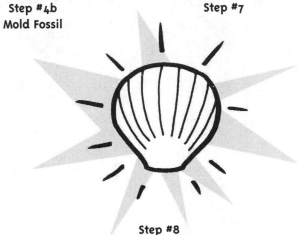

Step #8
Cast Fossil

 Activity Goals

To make mold and cast fossils. To demonstrate how some fossils are formed in nature.

 Earth Note

Mold and cast fossils are imprints of only the hard parts of plants and animals.

 Key to Success

Cover the work surface. Use clay that doesn't need to be used again. The clay needs to be pliable for small hands.

 Hint

If you don't have clay, plaster of paris paste can be used for both the mold and the cast.

11   Trace Fossils—Form a Burrow

Did you know?

Trace fossils record the activities of an animal. Trace fossils can include the burrow, trail, and tracks left behind by an animal.

You will need

Small paper cup containing damp sand
Pencil
Small plastic cup
Plaster of paris
Water
Hard plastic table knife

Now you are ready to

1. Push the pencil into the sand. You have now made a burrowlike shape with the pencil. Leave the pencil in the sand.
2. Make a small portion of plaster of paris paste in the plastic cup. You will need 2 tablespoons of plaster of paris and 1 tablespoon of water for one burrow. Pour the water in first and then pour the plaster of paris into the water. Let it sit for 2 minutes.
3. Stir the plaster mixture with the hard plastic knife. The mixture should be somewhat thick.
4. Take the pencil out. Pour enough plaster of paris paste into the burrowlike hole to fill it to the top. You may need to use the knife to get the plaster mixture out of the cup.
5. When the plaster has hardened, usually the next day, pull it out of the sand. This is the tracing of the burrow made by your pencil as it moved through the sand. It will be a white "fossil" coated with sand.

Brain exercise

When I looked at the pencil burrow, I thought . . .

Trace Fossil

12   Name That Fossil! Bingo

Did you know?

Fossils can be as large as a huge dinosaur skeleton or as tiny as microscopic plants and animals.

You will need

Name That Fossil! Bingo Board, page 73, copied onto card stock

Name That Fossil! Picture Cards, page 74, copied onto card stock

Scissors

Answers, page 180

Now you are ready to

1. Cut out all the picture cards.
2. Look at your Name That Fossil! Bingo Board. Find the picture card that you think goes with each name on the board.
3. Check the answers on page oo to see how many fossils you matched correctly.
4. Did you make a bingo?
5. Try making a bingo again later and see how much you've learned.

 Activity Goal

To identify eight different fossils.

 Earth Note

Only a small percentage of the plants and animals that have lived on Earth are eventually preserved as fossils.

 Key to Success

This game works well after children have had a chance to get to know each fossil. Readers and nonreaders should pair up.

 Hint

Children love testing their knowledge. It won't be long before they can match all of the fossil names to their pictures.

Name That Fossil! Bingo Board

1 ancient shark tooth	**2** amber	**3** ammonite
4 fossil snail	**5** Fossil Board	**6** dinosaur bone
7 trilobite	**8** belemnite	**9** dinosaur eggshell

Name That Fossil! Picture Cards

13 Fossil Fuel Products Scavenger Hunt

Did you know?

Fossil fuels come from the remains of ancient plants and some ancient animals. Coal and oil are fossil fuels. Many of the things you wear are made from fossil fuels. Some lipstick, crayons, shoe polish, ink, and clothing contain ingredients from ancient fossils.

You will need

Fossil Fuel Products Scavenger Hunt Board, page 76, copied onto card stock

Scissors

Pencil

Now you are ready to

1. Cut out the Fossil Fuel Products Scavenger Hunt Board.
2. Check your home and school for items listed on the board.
3. Once you find an item, place a checkmark in its square.
4. Did you find all of the items?

Brain exercise

When I looked for items on my scavenger hunt, I . . .

 Activity Goal

To identify products made using fossil fuels.

 Earth Note

When you drive in a car, you are burning fossil fuels. Burning fossil fuels causes air pollution.

 Key to Success

This scavenger hunt is a fun individual, partner, or team activity. Nonreaders should pair up with readers.

 Hint

To take this activity one step further, discuss pollution caused by burning fossil fuels. Ask children to brainstorm pollution-cutting ideas.

Fossil Fuel Products Scavenger Hunt Board

polyester clothing	rubber-soled shoes	nail polish
shoe polish	crayons	petroleum jelly
sunglasses	plastic toy	free choice

How the Earth Works, ©2002. Published by Chicago Review Press, Inc., 800-888-7471.

Revealing Rocks and Minerals

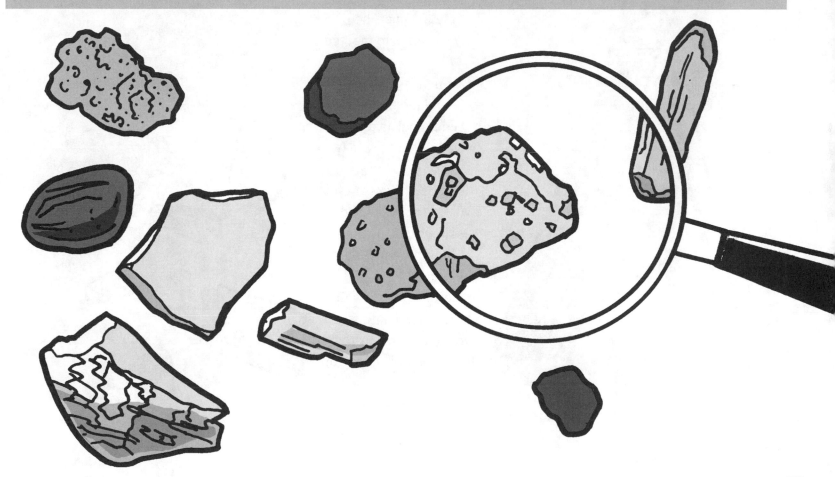

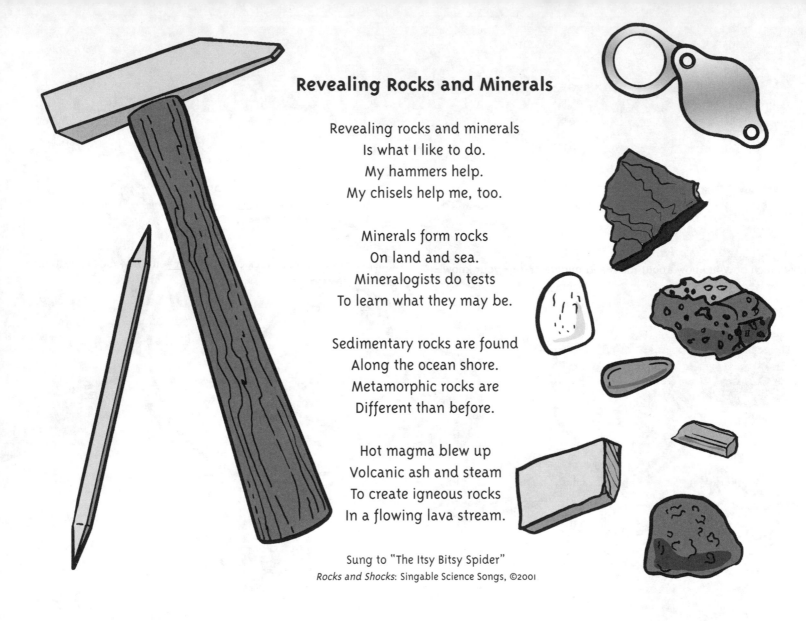

Revealing Rocks and Minerals

Revealing rocks and minerals
Is what I like to do.
My hammers help.
My chisels help me, too.

Minerals form rocks
On land and sea.
Mineralogists do tests
To learn what they may be.

Sedimentary rocks are found
Along the ocean shore.
Metamorphic rocks are
Different than before.

Hot magma blew up
Volcanic ash and steam
To create igneous rocks
In a flowing lava stream.

Sung to "The Itsy Bitsy Spider"
Rocks and Shocks: Singable Science Songs, ©2001

In Revealing Rocks and Minerals you will find

Wonderful Words from Revealing Rocks and Minerals

Geologists   These scientists study rocks and minerals to learn more about Earth's history and structure.

Geology   Geology is the study of what Earth is made of and how its structure changes over time.

Igneous Rock   This type of rock is formed when hot liquid magma cools and becomes solid.

Magnetic   When an object is attracted to a magnet or can be magnetized, it is called magnetic.

Metamorphic Rock   Sedimentary or igneous rocks can be changed by Earth's heat, pressure, or chemical reactions into new kinds of rocks. These new rocks are called metamorphic, which means "changed into a new shape."

Mineralogist   This is a scientist who studies rocks and minerals.

Minerals   Minerals are rock ingredients, or the building blocks of rocks.

Mohs' Scale of Hardness   This scale rates the hardness of minerals from 1, the softest, to 10, the hardest. A scientist named Frederich Mohs developed it in 1822 as a way to help identify different minerals. Mohs' Scale of Hardness is still used today.

Molten   This word means "melted."

Properties   Properties help you tell the difference between one thing and another. Color, shape, hardness, texture, and sometimes magnetism are all properties of minerals and rocks.

Rocks   Rocks are combinations of one or more minerals.

Sedimentary Rock   When layers of mud, ground-up rock, clay, and sometimes fossils of plants or shells harden or cement together, they become sedimentary rock. Fossils are most commonly found in sedimentary rock such as limestone or shale.

Sediments   These are layers of mud, clay, and ground-up grains of rock that collect on the bottom of rivers, lakes, or oceans.

Specimen   A specimen is a sample of the rock or fossil you are studying.

Dynamic Earth

What should I know about rocks and minerals?

● Geologists study rocks and minerals to learn about Earth's history and structure. Although Earth was formed at least 4.5 billion years ago, rocks are not that old. Earth's heat, pressure, and movements are constantly changing old rocks into new rocks.

● Minerals are the building blocks of rocks. Combinations of one or more minerals form rocks. There are at least 2,000 named and identified minerals.

● There are three types of rocks. Rocks can be igneous, sedimentary, or metamorphic. *Igneous* means "made by fire." Igneous rocks are formed when molten magma cools and becomes solid. Some igneous rocks, such as granite, are formed deep within Earth's crust, while others, such as pumice, are formed when magma erupts from a volcano and turns into lava. When the lava cools, it forms solid igneous rocks.

● *Sedimentary* means "settled down." Naturally cemented layers of mud and sand form sedimentary rock. Sedimentary rock can contain the fossil remains of animals and plants. Fossils are most commonly found in sedimentary rock such as limestone and shale.

● Rock that is formed when sedimentary or igneous rocks are changed by Earth's heat, pressure, or chemical reactions is called *metamorphic*.

● Geologists and mineralogists identify minerals by their properties. These properties include color, shape, hardness, texture, and sometimes magnetism. Mohs' Scale of Hardness is used to rate minerals from the softest to the hardest. The streak test helps identify some minerals by the colored powder they leave behind when they are rubbed against a streak plate. Talcum is the softest mineral, whereas diamond is the hardest mineral. Some minerals are magnetic. Mineralogists and geologists perform many tests to help them identify minerals.

1 Best Guess—Rocks and Minerals Trivia Cards

Did you know?
Geology is the scientific study of Earth's history and structure.

You will need
2 sheets (8½ × 11 inches) light-colored card stock

Rocks and Minerals Trivia Card Fronts, page 84, copied onto 1 sheet of card stock

Rocks and Minerals Trivia Card Backs, page 85, copied onto 1 sheet of card stock

Scissors

Glue

Partner

Rubber band

What do you think?
If I try to guess the answers for the Rocks and Minerals Trivia questions, I will guess ___ out of 4 correctly.

Now you are ready to
1. Cut out the 16 Rocks and Minerals Trivia cards from both sheets of card stock.
2. Match the card fronts to their answer backs. Glue the matching card pieces together, back-to-back. Laminate the cards if you like.
3. Place the cards with the question side up.
4. Ask your partner to give a best-guess answer to the first four questions. Once a question is answered, check the back of the card to see if it was answered correctly. How well did your partner guess?
5. Next, it is your turn to guess the answers to the last four cards. How well did you guess?
6. When you are finished, wrap a rubber band around the cards to keep them together.

Brain exercise
When I guessed the answers, I felt . . .

Activity Goal	**Earth Note**	**Key to Success**	**Hint**
To learn new information about rocks and minerals in a fun trivia card game.	Geologists identify minerals by their properties. Rocks are made up of one mineral or a combination of minerals.	One partner needs to be able to read. Some children may need help cutting out and gluing the cards.	Children love playing with the trivia cards. It's a fun way for them to learn new things and test their knowledge.

Rocks and Minerals Trivia Card Fronts

Rocks and Minerals Trivia ①	Rocks and Minerals Trivia ②	Rocks and Minerals Trivia ③	Rocks and Minerals Trivia ④
What rock is sometimes called fool's gold?	Geologists are scientists who study rocks and minerals to learn more about the history of _____?	What are the building blocks of rocks?	What type of rock is made up of layered sediments?

Rocks and Minerals Trivia ⑤	Rocks and Minerals Trivia ⑥	Rocks and Minerals Trivia ⑦	Rocks and Minerals Trivia ⑧
What type of rock has changed through heat or pressure?	What type of rock's name means "made by fire"?	There are at least how many named and identified minerals?	What is the hardest mineral?

How the Earth Works, ©2002. Published by Chicago Review Press, Inc., 800-888-7471.

Rocks and Minerals Trivia Card Backs

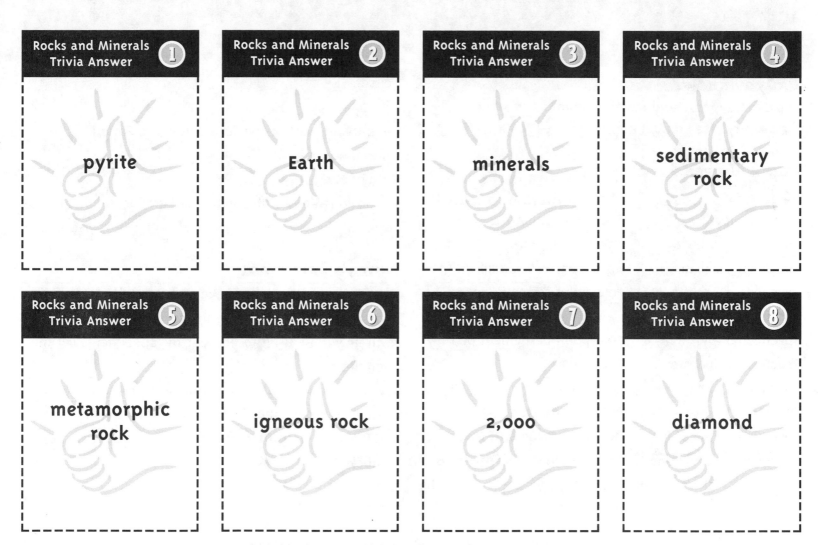

Rocks and Minerals Trivia Answer ①	**Rocks and Minerals Trivia Answer** ②	**Rocks and Minerals Trivia Answer** ③	**Rocks and Minerals Trivia Answer** ④
pyrite	Earth	minerals	sedimentary rock
Rocks and Minerals Trivia Answer ⑤	**Rocks and Minerals Trivia Answer** ⑥	**Rocks and Minerals Trivia Answer** ⑦	**Rocks and Minerals Trivia Answer** ⑧
metamorphic rock	igneous rock	2,000	diamond

Did you know?

You can buy rocks and minerals from stores around the country. See Product Information, page 181.

You will need

Adult helper

Specimen 1, calcite

Specimen 2, quartz

Specimen 3, talcum

Specimen 4, apatite

Specimen 5, hematite

Specimen 6, pyrite

Specimen 7, lodestone

Specimen 8, limestone

Specimen 9, granite

Specimen 10, mica

Specimen 11, sandstone

Specimen 12, shale

Specimen 13, slate

Specimen 14, marble

Specimen 15, pumice

Specimen 16, obsidian

Fine-point correction pen (white ink)

Fine-point permanent pen (black ink)

4 sheets (8½ × 11 inches) light-colored card stock

Rocks and Minerals Information Cards (pages 88, 89, 90, and 91) copied onto the card stock

Scissors

Glue

Magnifying glass or jeweler's loupe (see Product Information, page 181)

Rubber band

Plastic lidded case with dividers (see Product Information, page 181) or large empty egg carton with cotton padding

Now you are ready to

1. With an adult's help, make a very small white circle on each specimen, using the correction pen. This circle will be used to number the specimens. Let the circles dry.

2. Ask an adult to use the permanent pen to write each specimen's number (listed above) in its white circle.

3. Cut out the information cards from the sheets of card stock.

4. Match the information card fronts to their backs. Glue the matching card pieces together, back-to-back. Laminate the cards if you like.
5. Use the magnifying glass to examine each specimen.
6. Read the information cards to learn more about each specimen.
7. When you are finished with this activity, wrap a rubber band around the cards to keep them together. Put the information cards and the specimens in your rocks and minerals case.

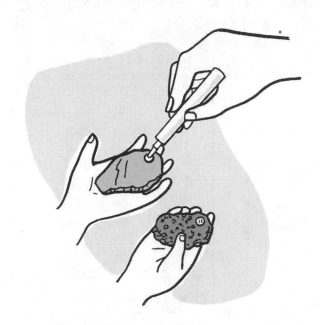

 Activity Goal

To collect and store rocks and minerals.

 Earth Note

Many rocks and minerals are very old. They need to be handled carefully and treated with great respect.

 Key to Success

The white circles with the numbers should be very small and unobtrusive. Place the rocks and minerals case at a learning center where children can explore each specimen.

 Hint

In the future, if you wish to remove the ink from a specimen, use fingernail polish remover. If you are unable to find or purchase the minerals and rocks, go to your nearest natural history museum to view their minerals and rocks.

Rocks and Minerals Information Card Fronts

Specimen 1

Specimen 2

Specimen 3

Specimen 4

Specimen 5

Specimen 6

Specimen 7

Specimen 8

How the Earth Works, ©2002. Published by Chicago Review Press, Inc., 800-888-7471.

Rocks and Minerals Information Card Fronts

Specimen 9

Specimen 10

Specimen 11

Specimen 12

Specimen 13

Specimen 14

Specimen 15

Specimen 16

Rocks and Minerals Information Card Backs

Rocks and Minerals Information Card 1

calcite

A very common mineral, calcite is found in many rocks. It is the only mineral that fizzes when placed in vinegar. (Hardness —3)

Rocks and Minerals Information Card 2

quartz

One of the most common minerals in Earth's crust, quartz is found in many igneous rocks. (Hardness —7)

Rocks and Minerals Information Card 3

talcum

A metamorphic rock, talcum, or talc, is one of the softest minerals. (Hardness —1)

Rocks and Minerals Information Card 4

apatite

This mineral has many forms and colors. (Hardness —5)

Rocks and Minerals Information Card 5

hematite

Hematite contains mostly iron. It is the most important iron ore.

Rocks and Minerals Information Card 6

pyrite

This type of iron ore is sometimes called fool's gold.

Rocks and Minerals Information Card 7

lodestone

A form of the mineral magnetite, lodestone is a natural magnet.

Rocks and Minerals Information Card 8

limestone

A sedimentary rock, limestone often has fossils in it. Limestone consists mainly of the mineral calcite.

Rocks and Minerals Information Card Backs

Rocks and Minerals
Information Card 9
granite
A common igneous rock, granite is often used in buildings and monuments.

Rocks and Minerals
Information Card 10
mica
A mineral that is paper-thin, mica also forms in metamorphic rocks.

Rocks and Minerals
Information Card 11
sandstone
A sedimentary rock, sandstone is formed by wind, water, and glaciers.

Rocks and Minerals
Information Card 12
shale
A sedimentary rock, shale is made of hardened clay.

Rocks and Minerals
Information Card 13
slate
A metamorphic rock, slate was once shale.

Rocks and Minerals
Information Card 14
marble
A metamorphic rock, marble was once limestone.

Rocks and Minerals
Information Card 15
pumice
An igneous rock, pumice is very light-weight and can float on water. Pumice is sometimes called volcanic froth.

Rocks and Minerals
Information Card 16
obsidian
An igneous rock, obsidian is some-times called volcanic glass.

How the Earth Works, ©2002. Published by Chicago Review Press, Inc., 800-888-7471.

3 Mineral Identification I—Scratch It!

Did you know?

Geologists use hardness to help them identify minerals. Mohs' Scale of Hardness rates how hard a mineral is on a scale of 1 to 10. Hardness is usually measured by seeing how easy it is to scratch a mineral.

You will need

Adult helper

Penny

1 opened metal paper clip

Scratch Test Results form, page 94, copied onto white paper

1 Mohs' Scale of Hardness, page 94, copied onto white paper

Specimens from Rocks and Minerals Collection Starter, activity #2, page 86

     Specimen 1

     Specimen 3

     Specimen 4

Answers, page 180

Rocks and minerals case

Empty baby food jar

What do you think?

If I test the hardness of a mineral, I (will) or (won't) be able to identify it correctly.

Now you are ready to

1. Place the penny, opened metal paper clip, and baby food jar on the table. Place your Scratch Test Results form on the table with your copy of Mohs' Scale of Hardness.

2. Try to scratch each specimen with your fingernail. If your fingernail scratched the specimen, mark 0 in its fingernail box on your Scratch Test Results form. If it did not scratch the specimen, mark X.

3. Try to scratch each specimen with the penny. If the penny scratched the specimen, mark 0 in its penny box on your Scratch Test Results form. If it did not scratch the specimen, mark X.

4. Try to scratch each specimen with the paper clip. If the paper clip scratched the specimen, mark 0 in its paper clip box on your Scratch Test Results form. If it did not scratch the specimen, mark X.

5. Look at your completed Scratch Test Results form. Which specimen has no Xs in its boxes? This is the softest of the three mineral specimens. Check Mohs' Scale of Hardness and write the name of the mineral you think it might be.

6. Look at your completed Scratch Test Results form. Which specimen has two Xs in its boxes? This is the hardest of the three mineral specimens. Check Mohs' Scale of Hardness and write the name of the mineral you think it might be.

7. Look at your completed Scratch Test Results form. Which specimen has one X in its boxes? Check Mohs' Scale of Hardness and write the name of the mineral it might be.

8. Now check the answers on page 180 to see if you identified the specimens correctly.

9. When you are finished with this activity, be sure to place the specimens back in your rocks and minerals case. Place the penny and paper clip in the baby food jar so others can try this activity later.

Brain exercise
When I scratched the specimens with my fingernail, I . . .

 Activity Goal

To conduct a scratch test to identify three minerals.

 Earth Note

The hardest mineral is diamond. It scratches anything.

 Key to Success

Children need to be able to spend enough time with each mineral.

 Hint

This is a great team activity. If you do this in teams, you will need one sample of each specimen and one set of scratch tools per group.

Mohs' Scale of Hardness

Mineral	Hardness (from 1 to 10)	Test for Hardness
talcum	1	Can be scratched by anything, even a fingernail.
gypsum	2	
calcite	3	Can be scratched by a penny.
fluorite	4	Can be scratched by a paper clip.
apatite	5	
orthoclase	6	Can scratch steel and glass.
quartz	7	
topaz	8	
corundum	9	Scratches most materials.
diamond	10	

Scratch Test Results

Test for Hardness

Specimen	Fingernail	Penny	Paper Clip
1			
3			
4			

4 Mineral Identification II—Streak It!

Did you know?

A streak test is one of the tests used in identifying minerals. Minerals leave their own special powdery trail, called a streak, when they are rubbed on a porous surface.

You will need

Light-colored ceramic tile (use the flat porous back of the tile as your streak plate)

Flat work surface

Colored chalk (chalk is calcite)

Specimens from Rocks and Minerals Collection Starter, activity #2, on page 86

        Specimen 5, hematite (red streak)

        Specimen 3, talcum (white, chalky streak)

        Specimen 6, pyrite (greenish-black streak)

Any other specimens you want to test

Rocks and minerals case

What do you think?

If I rub hematite across a tile, it (will) or (won't) leave a black streak.

Now you are ready to

1. Carefully place the tile upside down on the work surface. Using the flat porous back of the tile, rub the colored chalk against the tile. Did it make a streak, or line, on the tile? If so, what color was its streak?

2. Rub the hematite (specimen 5) against the tile. Did it make a streak on the tile? If so, what color was its streak?

3. Rub the talcum (specimen 3) against the tile. Did it make a streak on the tile? If so, what color was its streak?

4. Rub the pyrite (specimen 6) against the tile. Did it make a streak on the tile? If so, what color was its streak?

5. Try rubbing other minerals or rocks you find against the tile. Which streaks did you like the best?

6. When you are finished with this activity, be sure to place the specimens back in your rocks and minerals case.

Brain exercise

When I rubbed a mineral against the streak plate, I . . .

 Activity Goal

To demonstrate the use of a streak test in identifying minerals.

 Earth Note

Chalk leaves a powdery streak on a chalkboard. Chalk is made of the mineral calcite.

 Key to Success

Use a light-colored tile piece with a flat porous back.

 Hint

Talcum leaves a white, powdery streak, but it's harder to see than a darker-colored streak. Use a magnifying glass or light source to see it better.

5 Mineral Identification III—Is It Magnetic?

Did you know?
Magnetic properties are found in minerals that contain iron and cobalt.

You will need

Magnet

Metal paper clip

Specimens from Rocks and Minerals Collection Starter, activity #2, page 86

Specimen 2, quartz

Specimen 4, apatite

Specimen 7, lodestone

Rocks and Minerals case

What do you think?
Lodestone has a mineral in it called magnetite. Magnetite contains iron. If I place lodestone near a magnet, the lodestone (will) or (won't) be attracted to the magnet.

Now you are ready to
1. Place the metal paper clip near the magnet. What happens? Is the paper clip magnetic?
2. Place the quartz (specimen 2) near the magnet. What happens? Is the quartz magnetic?
3. Place the apatite (specimen 4) near the magnet. What happens? Is the apatite magnetic?
4. Place the lodestone (specimen 7) near the magnet. What happens? Is the lodestone magnetic?
5. Try testing other rocks and minerals to see if they are magnetic. How many did you find that were magnetic?
6. When you are finished with this activity, be sure to place the specimens back in your rocks and minerals case.

Brain exercise
When I used the magnet, I . . .

Activity Goal

To identify rocks and minerals with magnetic properties.

Earth Note

Magnetism is one more tool that can be used in mineral and rock identification.

Key to Success

This works very well as a partner activity.

Hint

This activity is great fun. Children enjoy using magnets on any rocks.

6 Mineral Identification IV—Dip It!

Did you know?

One of the most common minerals on Earth is calcite. Calcite fizzes when it is put into vinegar. This is a very good way to identify calcite.

You will need

4 clear plastic cups	Specimen 1, calcite
Vinegar	Specimen 8, limestone
Chalk	Specimen 9, granite
Specimens from Rocks and	Magnifying glass
Minerals Collection Starter,	Rocks and minerals case
activity #2, page 86	

What do you think?

If I place chalk in vinegar, it (will) or (won't) make bubbles.

Now you are ready to

1. Pour vinegar into one of the clear plastic cups. Drop a piece of chalk into it. What is happening to the vinegar? Can you see bubbles? If you can see bubbles coming up from the chalk, you know it has the mineral calcite in it.

2. Pour vinegar into another one of the clear plastic cups. Drop a piece of calcite (specimen 1) into it. What is happening to the vinegar? Do you see any bubbles in the vinegar?

3. Pour vinegar into a third clear plastic cup. Drop a piece of limestone (specimen 8) into it. What is happening to the vinegar? Can you see bubbles? Do you think the limestone has calcite in it?

4. Pour vinegar into the fourth clear plastic cup. Drop a piece of granite (specimen 9) into it. What is happening to the vinegar? Can you see bubbles? Do you think the granite has calcite in it?

5. Use a magnifying glass to take a closer look.

6. When you are finished with this activity, be sure to place the specimens back in your rocks and minerals case.

Brain exercise

When I looked at the chalk in the vinegar, I thought . . .

Activity Goal	**Earth Note**	**Key to Success**	**Hint**
To observe the reaction of calcite when it is placed in vinegar.	Chalk is made of the mineral calcite.	Geologists usually use a stronger acid than the acetic acid in vinegar. Bubbles will show when calcite is present, but children may need to use a magnifying glass. Pour the vinegar out of the cups within 30 minutes.	An adult must be present when children are using vinegar. Try placing a seashell in vinegar for a few days.

7 Favorite Ingredients—Rocks and Cookies

Did you know?
Minerals are the ingredients of rocks.

You will need
1 large chocolate chip cookie

1 large oatmeal raisin cookie

1 lunch sack containing the following:

> Flour (small sample in a resealable plastic bag)
>
> Butter (small sample in a resealable plastic bag)
>
> 1 sugar cube or sugar packet
>
> 10 chocolate chips in a resealable plastic bag
>
> Oatmeal flakes with 10 raisins in a resealable plastic bag

Specimens from Rocks and Minerals Collection Starter, activity #2, page 86

> Specimen 9, granite
>
> Specimen 10, mica
>
> Specimen 2, quartz

Magnifying glass

Rocks and minerals case

What do you think?
If I look at a piece of granite, I (will) or (won't) be able to see the minerals that formed it.

Now you are ready to
1. Look at the chocolate chip cookie. What do you predict are its ingredients?
2. Look at the oatmeal raisin cookie. What do you predict are its ingredients?
3. Empty the lunch sack onto the table. What do you find? Inside are some of the ingredients used to make the chocolate chip and oatmeal raisin cookies.
4. Minerals are the ingredients of rocks, just as flour, butter, and sugar are the ingredients of most cookies. Place the granite on the table. Look at the mica and the quartz. Both of these minerals are ingredients in the granite.

5. Use the magnifying glass to take a closer look at the mica and the quartz on the outside of the piece of granite. Can you see these minerals?

6. When you are finished with this activity, be sure to place the specimens back in your rocks and minerals case.

Brain exercise
When I looked at the granite, I thought . . .

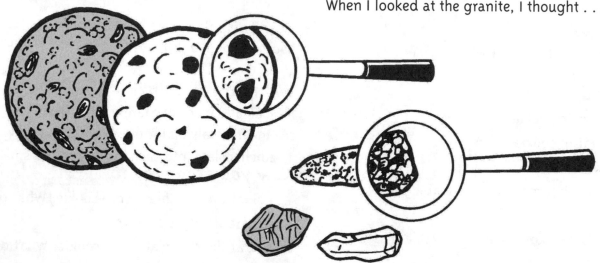

Activity Goals	**Earth Note**	**Key to Success**	**Hint**
To identify the ingredients in a chocolate chip and an oatmeal raisin cookie. To observe two minerals commonly found in granite.	Granite is one of the most common rocks found on Earth. Quartz is one of the most common minerals found in rock.	Use clear plastic resealable bags for your cookie ingredients.	If possible, make cookies with your children. Talk about how ingredients such as chocolate chips melt when they are baked to form the cookie.

8 Igneous Chocolate—"Made by Fire!"

Did you know?
Igneous means "made by fire." Igneous rocks are made when molten magma cools.

You will need
Adult helper

1 package candy-making chocolates

1 16-ounce glass measuring cup with pour spout

Microwave

Oven mitt

Plastic candy mold

What do you think?
If I pour melted chocolate into a mold, it (will) or (won't)

become solid when it cools down.

Now you are ready to
1. Fill the measuring cup with the chocolates.
2. Microwave the chocolates until they are liquid.
3. With an adult's help, use the oven mitt to pour the melted chocolate into each mold. Can you smell the chocolate odor? The melted chocolates release an invisible gas.
4. When the chocolate has cooled, pop the candies out of the mold. Repeat until everyone has a piece of chocolate.

Brain exercise
When the chocolate cooled down, it . . .

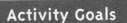 **Activity Goals**

To observe solid, liquid, and gas states. To demonstrate the process that hot molten rock goes through to become solid.

Earth Note

Granite cools beneath Earth's crust, and pumice cools above.

 Key to Success

If you don't have enough chocolate for everyone, consider making only one sample piece for observation.

 Hint

Candy-making chocolates and molds are available at most craft stores.

9 Igneous Rock Collection Card

Did you know?

Pumice is sometimes called volcanic froth. It is an igneous rock that is so light it can float on water.

You will need

Igneous Rock Collection Card, page 105, copied onto card stock

Flat surface such as a desk or table

Rocks and Minerals Information Cards 9, 15, and 16

Specimens from Rocks and Minerals Collection Starter, activity #2, page 86

Specimen 9, granite

Specimen 15, pumice

Specimen 16, obsidian

Magnifying glass

Now you are ready to

1. Place the Igneous Rock Collection Card on the table.
2. Read the information cards for specimens 9, 15, and 16.
3. Match each specimen to its name on the Igneous Rock Collection Card.
4. Use a magnifying glass to take a closer look at the three igneous rocks.
5. Display your rocks on the Igneous Rock Collection Card.

 Activity Goals

To examine and compare igneous rocks. To identify and display igneous rocks.

 Earth Note

Obsidian is sometimes called volcanic glass because of its glasslike appearance.

 Key to Success

Read about igneous rocks in the chapter introduction before you do this activity.

 Hint

Use the book *Rocks and Minerals* (see page 182) to help identify and learn more about igneous rocks.

Sedimentary Rock Collection Card	limestone	sandstone	shale

Metamorphic Rock Collection Card	marble	talcum	slate

Igneous Rock Collection Card	pumice	granite	obsidian

10　It's Sedimentary! Snap a Snickers

Did you know?

Most sedimentary rocks form in layers.

You will need

1 Snickers bar

1 resealable plastic bag

Specimen 12, shale, from
Rocks and Minerals Collection

Starter, activity #2, page 86

Magnifying glass

Rocks and minerals case

What do you think?

If I snap a Snickers bar in half, I (will) or (won't) be able
to see the layers inside.

Now you are ready to

1. Unwrap the Snickers bar and snap it in half. How many
   layers do you see? Try to imagine that the nut layer is
   really made of fossils.
2. Place the candy bar in the resealable plastic bag for
   future viewing.
3. Look at specimen 12 (shale). Shale is a sedimentary rock.
   Does it have layers?
4. When you are finished with this activity, be sure to place
   the specimen back in your rocks and minerals case.

Brain exercise

When I snapped the Snickers, it . . .

 Activity Goal

To identify layers in a
candy bar and in a
piece of shale.

 Earth Note

Fossils are most often
found in sedimentary
rock such as shale or
limestone.

 Key to Success

Remind children that
the learning center
candy bar is for view-
ing, not eating.

 Hint

The children love snap-
ping their own Snickers
bars and then eating
them after viewing.

11 Sedimentary Rock Collection Card

Did you know?
Limestone is a sedimentary rock made mainly of the mineral calcite.

You will need
Sedimentary Rock Collection Card, page 105, copied onto card stock

Flat surface such as a desk or table

Rocks and Minerals Information Cards 8 and 12

Specimens from Rocks and Minerals Collection Starter, activity #2, page 86

> Specimen 8, limestone
>
> Specimen 11, sandstone
>
> Specimen 12, shale

Magnifying glass

Now you are ready to
1. Place the Sedimentary Rock Collection Card on the table.
2. Read the information cards for specimens 8, 11, and 12.
3. Match each specimen to its name on the Sedimentary Rock Collection Card.
4. Use a magnifying glass to take a closer look at the three sedimentary rocks.
5. Display your rocks on the Sedimentary Rock Collection Card.

 Activity Goals

To examine and compare sedimentary rocks. To identify and display sedimentary rocks.

 Earth Note

Shale is a sedimentary rock that is made of hardened layers of clay.

 Key to Success

Read about sedimentary rocks in the chapter introduction before you do this activity.

 Hint

Use the book *Rocks and Minerals* (see page 182) to help identify and learn more about sedimentary rocks.

12 Metamorphic Bars

Did you know?
Metamorphic rocks change from one form to another through Earth's heat and pressure.

You will need
Adult helper

1 10-ounce package regular marshmallows

6 cups Rice Krispies

3 tablespoons butter or margarine

Large microwave-safe mixing bowl

Microwave

Wooden spoon

Cooking spray

13 × 9 × 2-inch baking dish

Waxed paper

Metal spatula

Makes 24 2-inch bars

Now you are ready to
1. Examine the marshmallows and the Rice Krispies. Do they look like Rice Krispie Treats?

2. Place the marshmallows and butter in the mixing bowl. With an adult's help, microwave them on HIGH for 2 minutes. What has happened to these ingredients?

3. Stir the marshmallow mixture with the wooden spoon. Microwave the mixture on HIGH for another minute.

4. Add the Rice Krispies. Stir with the wooden spoon. Make sure the marshmallow mixture coats all the cereal. How are the Rice Krispies changing?

5. Coat the baking pan bottom with the cooking spray. Use the wooden spoon to remove the Rice Krispies mixture from the bowl and place it into the pan.

6. Press down firmly on the mixture, using the waxed paper to spread it evenly in the pan.

7. Once the Rice Krispie mixture has cooled, use the metal spatula to cut 2 × 2-inch bars.

8. Notice how heat and pressure have changed the ingredients.

Brain exercise
When I mixed the Rice Krispies with the melted marshmallow mixture, it reminded me . . .

To demonstrate how heat and pressure can make substances change form. To show the similarities between metamorphic Rice Krispie bars and metamorphic rocks.

 Earth Note

Igneous, sedimentary, and metamorphic rocks can be changed through Earth's heat and pressure to form new metamorphic rocks.

 Key to Success

As children are making the bars, remind them of how heat and pressure are changing the separate ingredients into a new bar form.

 Hint

If you are working with a group of children, ask for a few volunteers to help make the bars in front of the group. Make sure every child gets a bar.

13   Metamorphic Rock Collection Card

Did you know?

Slate was the sedimentary rock shale before it became a metamorphic rock. Marble is a metamorphic rock made from the sedimentary rock limestone.

You will need

Metamorphic Rock Collection Card, page 105, copied onto card stock

Flat surface such as a desk or table

Rocks and Minerals Information Card numbers 3, 8, 12, 13, and 14

Specimens from Rocks and Minerals Collection Starter, activity #2, page 86

> Specimen 3, talcum
>
> Specimen 8, limestone
>
> Specimen 12, shale
>
> Specimen 13, slate
>
> Specimen 14, marble

Magnifying glass

Now you are ready to

1. Place the Metamorphic Rock Collection Card on the table.
2. Read information cards 3, 13, and 14.
3. Match each specimen to its name on the Metamorphic Rock Collection Card.
4. Use a magnifying glass to take a closer look at the three metamorphic rocks.
5. Compare sedimentary specimen 12 (shale) to your metamorphic specimen 13 (slate). Look at them both through the magnifying glass. How do they look the same? How do they look different?
6. Compare sedimentary specimen 8 (limestone) to your metamorphic specimen 14 (marble). Look at them both through the magnifying glass. How do they look the same? How do they look different?
7. Display your rocks on the Metamorphic Rock Collection Card.

Activity Goals	Earth Note	Key to Success	Hint
To examine and compare metamorphic rocks. To identify and display metamorphic rocks. To compare a metamorphic rock to its original sedimentary rock.	Marble is a metamorphic rock made from the sedimentary rock limestone.	Read about metamorphic rocks in the chapter introduction before you do this activity.	Use the book *Rocks and Minerals* (see page 182) to help identify and learn more about metamorphic rocks.

14 Name That Rock! Bingo

Did you know?

Geologists study rocks to learn more about the history of planet Earth. Rocks reveal the secrets of Earth's past.

You will need

Name That Rock! Bingo Board, page 114, copied onto card stock

Name That Rock Type! Word Cards, page 115, copied onto card stock

Scissors

Answers, page 180

Specimens from Rocks and Minerals Collection Starter, activity #2, page 86

    Specimen 3, talcum

    Specimen 8, limestone

    Specimen 9, granite

    Specimen 11, sandstone

    Specimen 12, shale

    Specimen 13, slate

    Specimen 14, marble

    Specimen 15, pumice

    Specimen 16, obsidian

Rocks and Minerals Information Cards for the specimens listed above

Rocks and minerals case

Now you are ready to

1. Cut out all of the word cards.
2. Look at your Name That Rock! Bingo Board. Find the Name That Rock Type! Word Card that you think goes with each name on the bingo board. For example, granite is an igneous rock. Place an igneous rock word card on top of granite.
3. Check the answers on page 180 to see how many rocks you matched correctly.

4. Did you make a bingo?
5. Try making a bingo again later and see how much you've learned.
6. Take the Name That Rock Type! Word Cards off the board. Try to match the real specimen to its name on the bingo board.
7. Check the information cards and the numbers on the rocks to see if you matched them correctly.
8. Did you make a bingo?
9. When you are finished with this activity, be sure to place the specimens and their information cards back in your rocks and minerals case.

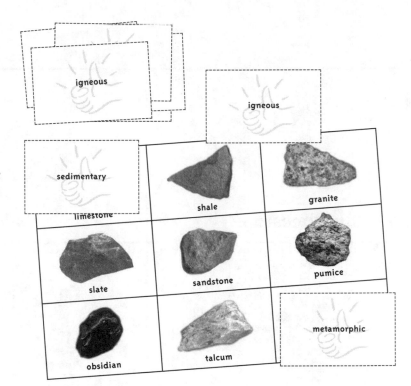

Activity Goal	**Earth Note**	**Key to Success**	**Hint**
To identify nine different rocks and the rock category in which they belong.	All rocks are either sedimentary, metamorphic, or igneous rocks.	This game works well after children have had a chance to get to know each rock type and specimen. Readers and nonreaders should pair up.	Children love testing their knowledge. It won't be long before they can match all of the rock names and types to their specimens.

Name That Rock! Bingo Board

limestone	shale	granite
slate	sandstone	pumice
obsidian	talcum	marble

Name That Rock Type! Word Cards

sedimentary	sedimentary	sedimentary
metamorphic	metamorphic	metamorphic
igneous	igneous	igneous

How the Earth Works, ©2002. Published by Chicago Review Press, Inc., 800-888-7471.

Crystals and Gems

Birthstones

January red—garnet's you!
February purple—amethyst true.
March—aquamarine blue.
I really like my birthstone.

April's diamond—clearly seen.
May's emerald—bright green.
June's pearl—translucent sheen.
I really like my birthstone.

July's ruby, fire-red glow.
August green is peridot.
September sapphire-blue shows.
I really like my birthstone.

October's opal rainbow bright.
November's topaz, a colorful sight.
December's turquoise-blue light.
I really like my birthstone.

Sung to "Skip to My Lou"
Rocks and Shocks: Singable Science Songs, ©2001

118

In Crystals and Gems you will find

Wonderful Words from Crystals and Gems

Crystals

Crystals are geometrically shaped mineral growths that can form as molten rock cools. Slow cooling makes well-formed crystals. Fast cooling makes poorly formed crystals.

Faces

Faces are the flat sides of a crystal. Crystals can have many faces or just a few. The faces can be different geometrical shapes.

Gems

Gems are minerals that have been specially cut and polished to show their beauty.

Gemstone

A gemstone is an especially beautiful and rare mineral that when cut and polished can be used as a jewel.

Lapidary

A person who cuts and polishes gemstones.

Mineralogist

A scientist who studies and identifies minerals.

Solution

A solution is formed when two different substances, such as sugar and water, are combined to form a new substance—sugar water. Usually a solution combines a liquid, such as water, and a solid, such as sugar or salt.

Dynamic Earth

What should I know about crystals and gems?

🌐 The word *crystal* comes from the Greek word *kyros*. Kyros means "icy cold." Long ago, people thought that quartz crystals were really ice that had frozen so hard it couldn't be thawed.

🌐 All crystals are unique. No two are exactly alike. They are usually symmetrical. One side of a crystal looks just like its other sides. Crystals have many flat surfaces, called *faces*.

🌐 Mineralogists are like detectives as they study clues to learn about and identify minerals. They use the mineral tests discussed in chapter 3 as well as other tests for identifying minerals.

🌐 A gemstone is an especially beautiful and rare mineral. When cut and polished, it can be used as a jewel in jewelry. Emeralds are gemstones known for their deep green color. Diamonds are known for their transparent brilliance. Opals are known for their rainbow of color and rubies for their fiery red appearance.

🌐 Beautiful stones such as turquoise and jade are made up of many crystals. They have been used in jewelry for more than 3,000 years. Topaz, amethyst, zircon, and peridot are less familiar gems. A lapidary is a person who cuts and polishes gemstones so they can be used in jewelry.

🌐 Birthstones have been worn for the past 2,000 years. Each month of the year has been given a birthstone. Do you know the name of the birthstone for the month in which you were born?

1 Crystals and Gems Fact or Fiction

Did you know?

Crystals and gems have been used in jewelry for thousands of years.

You will need

2 sheets (8½ × 11 inches) light-colored card stock

Crystals and Gems Fact or Fiction Card Fronts, page 124, copied onto 1 sheet of card stock

Crystals and Gems Fact or Fiction Card Backs, page 125, copied onto 1 sheet of card stock

Scissors

Glue

Partner

Rubber band

What do you think?

If I try to guess the answers for Crystals and Gems Fact or Fiction, I will guess __ out of 4 correctly.

Now you are ready to

1. Cut out the 16 Crystals and Gems Fact or Fiction cards from both sheets of card stock.
2. Match the card fronts to their answer backs. Glue the matching card pieces together, back-to-back. Laminate the cards if you like.
3. Place the cards with the answer sides down.
4. Ask your partner to guess fact or fiction to the first four cards. Each time your partner answers, check the back of the card to see if he or she was right. How well did your partner guess?
5. Next it is your turn to guess fact or fiction for the last four cards. How well did you guess?
6. When you are finished, wrap a rubber band around the cards to keep them together.

Brain exercise

When I guessed the answers, I . . .

 Activity Goal

To learn new information about crystals and gems in a fun fact or fiction card game.

 Earth Note

Mineralogists use crystal shapes to help them identify minerals.

 Key to Success

One partner needs to be able to read. Some children may need help cutting out and gluing the cards.

 Hint

Children love playing with the fact or fiction cards. These cards are a great way for children to learn new information and test their knowledge.

Crystals and Gems Fact or Fiction Card Fronts

Crystals and Gems Fact or Fiction ①

Diamonds are harder than any other material in nature.

Crystals and Gems Fact or Fiction ②

The largest diamond ever found weighed over 10 pounds.

Crystals and Gems Fact or Fiction ③

Almost all minerals have a crystal form.

Crystals and Gems Fact or Fiction ④

Mineralogists study minerals, gems, and crystals.

Crystals and Gems Fact or Fiction ⑤

Geodes are hollow stones with crystals inside.

Crystals and Gems Fact or Fiction ⑥

Turquoise was used in the earliest jewelry.

Crystals and Gems Fact or Fiction ⑦

Peridots are very famous jewels.

Crystals and Gems Fact or Fiction ⑧

Table salt crystals look just like Epsom salt crystals.

How the Earth Works, ©2002. Published by Chicago Review Press, Inc., 800-888-7471.

Crystals and Gems Fact or Fiction Card Backs

Crystals and Gems Fact or Fiction Answer ①	Crystals and Gems Fact or Fiction Answer ②	Crystals and Gems Fact or Fiction Answer ③	Crystals and Gems Fact or Fiction Answer ④
FACT	**FICTION** The largest diamond ever found weighed about 1 pound.	FACT	FACT

Crystals and Gems Fact or Fiction Answer ⑤	Crystals and Gems Fact or Fiction Answer ⑥	Crystals and Gems Fact or Fiction Answer ⑦	Crystals and Gems Fact or Fiction Answer ⑧
FACT	FACT	FICTION	FICTION

How the Earth Works, ©2002. Published by Chicago Review Press, Inc., 800-888-7471.

2 Crystals and Gems Collection Starter

Did you know?

Gems and crystals are available in rock and gem stores around the country. See Product Information, page 181.

You will need

Adult helper

Specimen 1, clear calcite

Specimen 2, amethyst

Fine-point correction pen (white ink)

Fine-point permanent pen (black ink)

The following, each in a clear resealable plastic bag:

    Specimen 3, table salt (1 tablespoon)

    Specimen 4, granulated sugar (1 tablespoon)

    Specimen 5, sea salt (1 tablespoon)

    Specimen 6, Epsom salt (1 tablespoon)

Magnifying glass

Plastic lidded case with dividers

Now you are ready to

1. With an adult's help, make a very small white circle on specimens 1 and 2 using the correction pen. Let the circles dry.
2. Ask an adult to use the permanent pen to write the specimen's number (listed above) in its white circle.
3. Label the plastic bags with each specimen's number.
4. Use the magnifying glass to examine each specimen.
5. When you are finished, place the specimens back in their case.

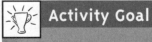 **Activity Goal**

To collect and store gemstones and crystals.

 Earth Note

Crystals and gemstones need to be handled carefully.

 Key to Success

Place the collection case at a learning center.

 Hint

Amethyst can be found in many craft and rock shops.

3 3-D Fun! Desktop Crystal Shape

Did you know?
Iron pyrite, or fool's gold, crystals are shaped like cubes.

You will need
Adult helper

Cube pattern, page 128, copied onto colored card stock

Scissors

Glue

Glitter

Ruler

Paper clip

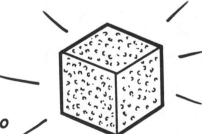

Now you are ready to
1. Cut out the cube pattern.

2. Decorate the unlined side of the cube pattern (inside the fold lines only) with glue and glitter to make it sparkle. This will become the outside of your cube.

3. Use the ruler and the paper clip to help you fold the pattern along each line. Then fold all the glue flaps toward the inside of the pattern.

4. Ask an adult to help you fold your cube. Together, fold the squares marked T upward. You hold the squares while the adult places glue dots on the outside of all flaps.

5. Fold the long piece up and around the two T squares. Glue the flaps to the inside of the pattern.

6. Press the last side against the remaining flaps.

7. When it is dry, display your cube in a special place.

 **Activity Goal**

To construct a three-dimensional crystal cube shape.

Earth Note

Table salt crystals and diamonds are cube shaped.

 Key to Success

Makes sure glitter doesn't get into the fold lines and glue flaps.

 Hint

Some children may need help folding the cube pattern.

Cube Pattern

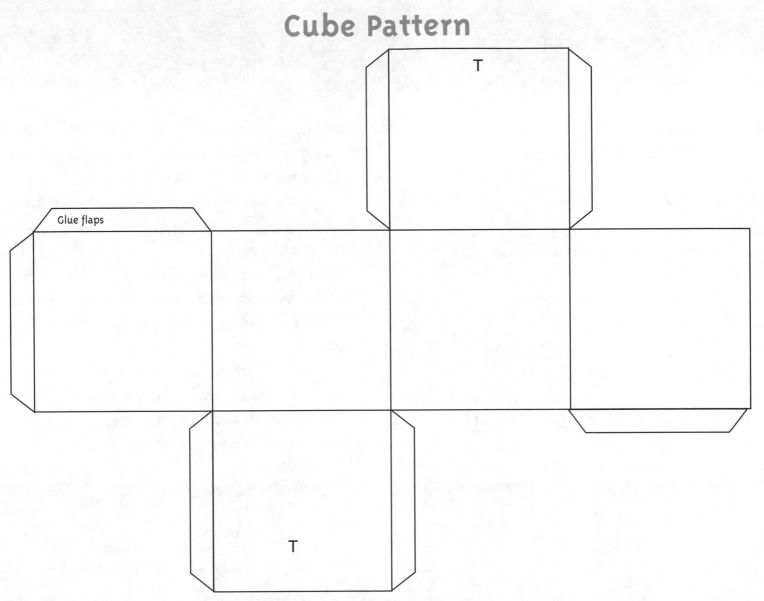

T

Glue flaps

T

4 Double Image? Curious Crystals

Did you know?

Calcite is the most common mineral on Earth.

You will need

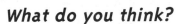

Black felt-tipped pen

Ruler

White index card

Specimen 1, calcite, from activity #2, page 126

Crystals and gems case

What do you think?

If I look at a line through a calcite crystal, I (will) or (won't) see double lines.

Now you are ready to

1. Using the ruler and pen, draw one dark line on the white index card.
2. Look at your line. Is it straight?
3. Place the calcite crystal on top of the line. How many lines can you see through the calcite?
4. When you are finished observing the calcite crystal, place it back in your crystals and gems case.

Brain exercise

When I looked at the line through calcite, I saw . . .

 Activity Goal

To observe the optical properties of a calcite crystal.

 Earth Note

Transparent calcite crystals are used in some microscopes.

 Key to Success

Make sure that the calcite is very clear, not opaque.

 Hint

This is a great partner activity.

5 Take a Closer Look I—Amazing Amethyst

Did you know?

Faces are the flat areas you see on a crystal.

You will need

Specimen 2, amethyst, from activity #2, page 126

Magnifying glass

Pencil

Paper

Crystals and gems case

What do you think?

If I examine an amethyst crystal, I (will) or (won't) be able to see faces on it.

Now you are ready to

1. Use the magnifying glass to take a closer look at the amethyst. Carefully touch and turn it all around. What color and shape is it? Is it hard or soft? Does it look sharp? Can you see through it at all?
2. How many faces can you count on your amethyst?
3. Do you know anyone with amethyst in a piece of jewelry?
4. Draw and write about the amethyst using the pencil and paper.
5. When you are finished looking at the amethyst specimen, place it back in your crystals and gems case.

Brain exercise

When I looked at the amethyst crystal, I saw . . .

 Activity Goal

To identify faces on an amethyst crystal.

 Earth Note

Amethyst is a form of quartz crystal.

 Key to Success

Amethysts can be somewhat sharp.

Hint

Children enjoy comparing the amethyst specimen to other crystals.

6 Take a Closer Look II—Everyday Crystals

Did you know?
Your home is filled with interesting crystals. You even eat some of them.

You will need
From activity #2, page 126

      Specimen 3, table salt

      Specimen 4, granulated sugar

      Specimen 5, sea salt

      Specimen 6, Epsom salt

Magnifying glass

Pencil

Paper

Crystals and gems case

What do you think?
If I look at a sample of sea salt, its crystals (will) or (won't) look the same as Epsom salt crystals.

Now you are ready to
1. Use the magnifying glass to take a closer look at the table salt crystals. What color and shape are they?
2. Look at the sugar crystals with the magnifying glass. What color and shape are they? Compare them to the table salt crystals.
3. Do you think that all the salt crystals will have the same shape? Using the magnifying glass, compare the sea salt and Epsom salt crystals.
4. Record your observations in writing and in drawings.
5. When you are finished looking at the specimens, place them back in your crystals and gems case.

Brain exercise
When I compared the salt crystals, I saw . . .

 Activity Goal

To compare and contrast common household crystals.

 Earth Note

Household crystals are in a processed form.

 Key to Success

Keep samples inside their resealable bags. They can be messy.

Hint

Sea salt should be available at your grocery store.

7 Alum Crystal Recipe

Did you know?

Alum is a mineral used in medicine and in pickle making.

You will need

Adult helper

1/4 cup alum

16-ounce glass measuring cup containing 1 cup hot tap water

1 hard plastic table knife

4 drops yellow food coloring

Index card

2 pencils

Large glass canning jar (found at grocery and craft stores)

Scissors

String

Pencil

Paper

Magnifying glass

What do you think?

If I pour an alum solution into a jar, crystals (will) or (won't) grow.

Now you are ready to

1. Pour the alum into the hot water in the measuring cup. Stir the mixture with the plastic table knife until the alum is dissolved.
2. Stir 4 drops of yellow food coloring into the liquid.
3. Write "alum" on the index card.
4. Pour the liquid into the jar.
5. Place the jar on top of the labeled index card in a location where it will be undisturbed for a week or more.
6. Cut the string long enough so that it will dip into the alum solution when hung from a pencil resting on the lip of the jar. Tie the string to the pencil.
7. Dip the string into the solution and rest the pencil on the jar's lip.

8. After 3 hours, check the solution. How does it look? Is anything happening? Record your observations using the pencil and paper.

9. Check the solution the next day. Record any changes.

10. Once a number of crystals have formed, collect them and observe them with the magnifying glass.

11. Place one of the alum crystals in your crystals and gems case.

Brain exercise

When I saw alum crystals growing, I thought . . .

🏆 Activity Goals

To grow crystals using an alum solution. To observe the properties of an alum crystal.

🌍 Earth Note

In nature, crystals take a very long time to grow.

👍 Key to Success

In order for alum crystals to grow, the water has to be hot. Follow the solution directions exactly.

✦ Hint

Children must be patient as they observe their crystals growing. Depending on the room temperature and other factors, crystals can take up to three weeks to grow.

8 Rock Candy Crystal Recipe

Did you know?

Every crystal is unique. No two crystals are exactly alike.

You will need

Adult helper

2 8-inch square, lightweight, disposable aluminum pans (found in grocery stores)

1 small nail

Roll of clean string

Scissors

Pot

1 cup water

2½ cups sugar

Wooden spoon

Stove

9-inch square of aluminum foil

Paper towel

Specimen 4, granulated sugar, from activity #2, page 126

Magnifying glass

Pencil

Paper

Special jar for rock candy

Crystals and gems case

What do you think?

If I pour a sugar solution into a pan, rock candy crystals (will) or (won't) grow.

Now you are ready to

1. With an adult's supervision, carefully use the nail to poke six holes 1 inch above the pan's bottom, evenly spaced, across one side of the pan. Poke six holes directly across from and on the opposite side of the pan, 1 inch above the pan bottom.

2. Lace the string through the holes. Tie a tight knot in the string on the outside of the pan, at the last hole.

Cut the string from the roll and tie a knot on the outside of the pan at the first hole.

3. Pour the water into the pot. Pour the sugar into the water. Stir with the wooden spoon until the sugar has dissolved. Cook the sugar mixture until it is syrupy.

4. Place the string-laced pan inside the unlaced pan to catch any leaking sugar solution. Place the pans in a location where they will be undisturbed.

5. Pour the syrup mixture into the laced pan. It needs to cover the strings.

6. Cover the top of the pan with the aluminum foil.

7. After 3 hours, check the sugar solution. How does it look? Is anything happening? Record your observations using the pencil and paper.

8. Check the solution the next day. Record your observations.

9. Once a number of crystals have formed on the strings, cut one of the strings, rinse the crystals lightly in cool water, and dry them on a paper towel. Observe some of the rock candy crystals through the magnifying glass. Do they look like the alum crystals?

10. Look at the granulated sugar with the magnifying glass. How is it similar to and different from the rock candy crystals made from it?

11. When you are ready to harvest your rock candy crystals, follow step 9. Taste a crystal, and then place the rock candy in a special jar.

12. Place a rock candy sample and the granulated sugar specimen in your crystals and gems case.

Brain exercise

When I tasted the rock candy crystals, I thought . . .

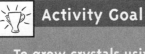 **Activity Goal**

To grow crystals using a sugar solution.

 Earth Note

The table sugar we use every day is made smooth and white by factories or processing plants.

 Key to Success

For best results, be sure that the strings are covered by almost an inch of syrup.

 Hint

Depending on the room temperature and other factors, rock candy crystals can take three or more weeks to grow.

9 Crystal Needle Recipe

Did you know?

Epsom salt comes from the mineral springs in Epsom, England.

You will need

Adult helper

Large glass canning jar

Enough clean pebbles to line the bottom of the jar

Index card

Pencil

Pan

$\frac{1}{2}$ cup water

1 cup Epsom salt

Stove

Wooden spoon

Magnifying glass

Specimen 6, Epsom salt, from activity #2, page 126

Pencil

Paper

Crystals and gems case

What do you think?

If I pour an Epsom salt solution into a jar, crystals (will) or (won't) grow.

Now you are ready to

1. Cover the inside bottom of the jar with different-sized pebbles.
2. Write "Epsom salt" on the index card.
3. Pour the water into the pan and add the Epsom salt. Ask an adult helper to bring the mixture to a boil, stirring the solution with the wooden spoon to dissolve the Epsom salt.
4. Pour the liquid into the jar.
5. Place the jar on top of the labeled index card in a location where it will be undisturbed for a few days.

6. After an hour, check the solution. How does it look? Is anything happening? Record your observations using the pencil and paper.

7. Check the solution after 2 hours and then again the next day.

8. Once a number of crystals have formed, observe them through the glass jar using the magnifying glass.

9. Look at the sample of the Epsom salt. Do these crystals look like the crystals growing on the rocks? How are they similar and how are they different?

10. Place an Epsom salt crystal sample and the Epsom salt specimen in your crystals and gems case.

Brain exercise

When I saw my Epsom salt crystals, I thought . . .

EPSOM SALT

 Activity Goals

To grow needle-shaped crystals using an Epsom salt solution. To observe the properties of Epsom salt crystals.

 Earth Note

Sometimes Epsom salt is used in a bath to help stop itching.

 Key to Success

The water has to boil for Epsom salt crystals to form. Follow the directions exactly.

 Hint

Epsom salt crystals seem to grow faster than many other types of crystals.

10 Salt Crystal Recipe

Did you know?

Table salt is used to season food and to preserve certain foods.

You will need

Adult helper

1/2 cup table salt

Glass measuring cup containing 3/4 cup warm tap water

1 hard plastic table knife

3 drops blue food coloring

Index card

2 pencils

Large glass canning jar

Scissors

String

Magnifying glass

Specimen 3, table salt, from activity #2, page 126

Paper

Crystals and gems case

What do you think?

If I pour a table salt solution into a jar, crystals (will) or (won't) grow.

Now you are ready to

1. Pour the table salt into the warm water in the cup. Stir the mixture with the plastic table knife until the salt is dissolved.
2. Stir 3 drops of blue food coloring into the liquid.
3. Write "table salt" on the index card.
4. Pour the liquid into the jar.
5. Place the jar on top of the labeled index card in a place where it will be undisturbed for a week or more.
6. Cut the string long enough so that it will dip into the table salt solution when hung from a pencil resting on the lip of the jar. Tie the string to the pencil.
7. Drop the string into the solution and rest the pencil on the jar's lip.

8. After 3 hours, check the solution. How does it look? Is anything happening? Record your observations using the paper and second pencil.

9. Check the solution the next day. Record your observations.

10. Once a number of crystals have formed, collect them and observe them with the magnifying glass.

11. Look at the table salt with the magnifying glass. Does the processed table salt look like the salt crystals growing in the jar? How are they similar and how are they different?

12. Place a table salt crystal sample and the table salt specimen in your crystals and gems case.

Brain exercise

When I made table salt crystals, I saw . . .

Activity Goals	**Earth Note**	**Key to Success**	**Hint**
To grow salt crystals using a table salt solution. To observe the properties of table salt crystals.	The table salt crystals we buy in stores are much smaller than the crystals we grow ourselves.	The water must be warm. Follow the solution directions exactly. Salt crystals can be difficult to grow.	Table salt crystals seem to take longer to grow than some other types of crystals.

11   My Birthstone Wheel

Did you know?

Birthstones have been worn as jewelry for 2,000 years.

You will need

Adult helper

Birthstone Wheel Front, page 141, copied onto card stock

Birthstone Wheel Back, page 142, copied onto card stock

Scissors

X-Acto knife

Bradley clip

Now you are ready to

1. Cut out the front and the back of the Birthstone Wheel.
2. Place the front circle on top of the back circle so that the writing shows through the cut-out triangle. Ask an adult to cut a very small X in the center of both circles using the X-Acto knife, cutting over the black center dot.
3. Push the bradley clip through the X in the two circles, fastening it behind the back circle.
4. Turn the top circle until you find the month in which you were born. What is the name of your birthstone?
5. Use the wheel to tell others what their birthstones are.

 Activity Goal

To identify the birthstones associated with each month of the year.

 Earth Note

Birthstones have been celebrated since biblical times.

 Key to Success

Make sure the circles line up properly.

 Hint

Children love this activity. Research each birthstone in an encyclopedia or gemstone book.

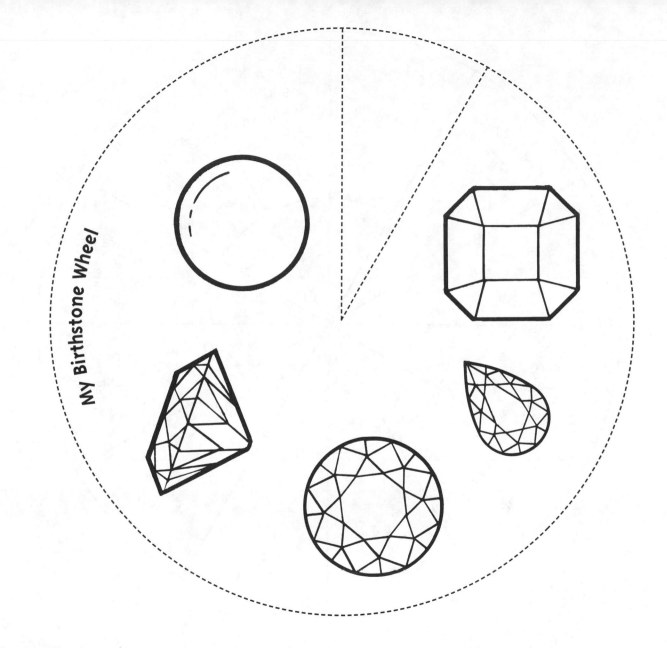

My Birthstone Wheel

How the Earth Works, ©2002. Published by Chicago Review Press, Inc., 800-888-7471.

Birthstone Wheel Back

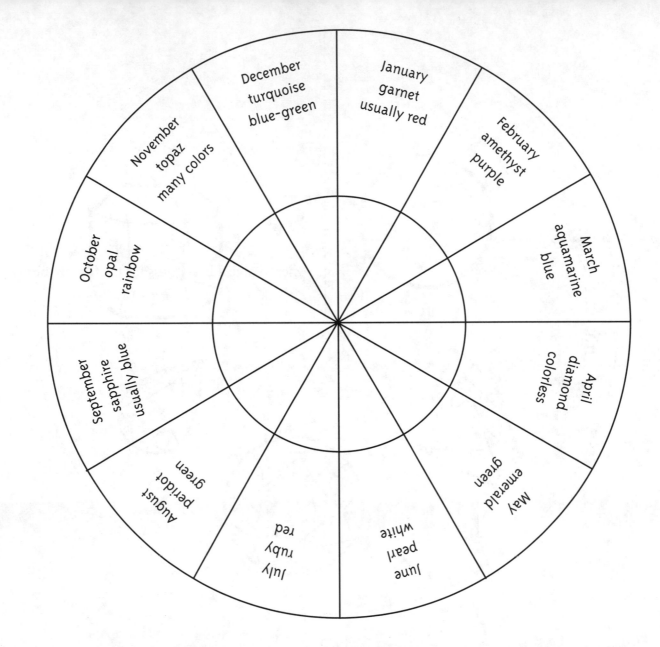

How the Earth Works, ©2002. Published by Chicago Review Press, Inc., 800-888-7471.

12 Birthstone Cards

Did you know?

April's birthstone is the hardest mineral.

You will need

Birthstone Card Fronts, pages 144 and 145, and Birthstone Card Backs, pages 146 and 147, copied onto white card stock (8½ × 11 inches)

Scissors

Glue

Partner

Rubber band

Now you are ready to

1. Cut out the 24 birthstone cards.
2. Match the birthstone card fronts to their backs. Glue the matching card pieces together, back-to-back.
3. Placing the cards with the month side up, ask your partner to give a best guess for the first six birthstones. Check the back of the card each time to see if the guess was correct.
5. Next, it is your turn to guess the last six birthstones. How well did you guess?
6. Use the rubber band to keep the cards together.

 Activity Goal

To learn information about each month's birthstone.

 Earth Note

Turquoise is found in some of the oldest jewelry.

 Key to Success

Laminating the cards helps to protect them from wear and tear.

 Hint

Discuss the birth months of people you know.

Birthstone Card Fronts

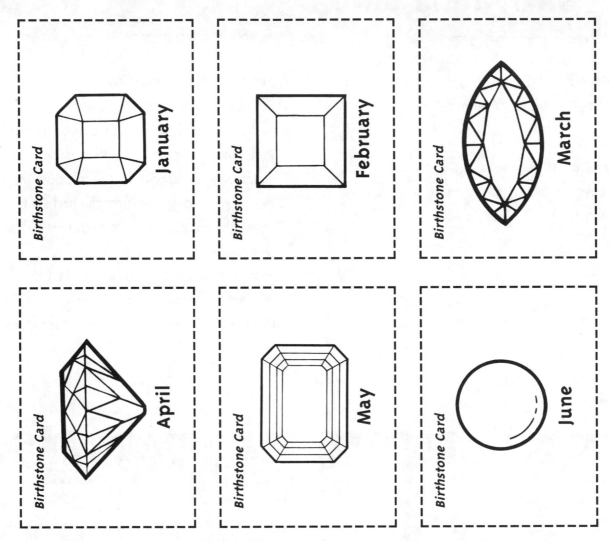

How the Earth Works, ©2002. Published by Chicago Review Press, Inc., 800-888-7471.

Birthstone Card Fronts

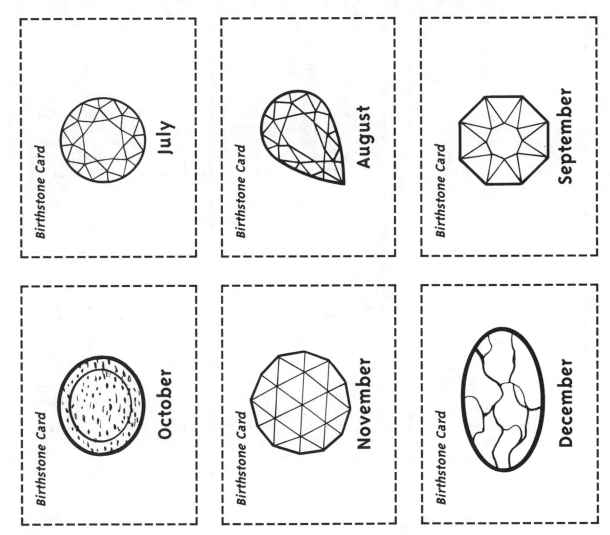

Birthstone Card — July

Birthstone Card — August

Birthstone Card — September

Birthstone Card — October

Birthstone Card — November

Birthstone Card — December

Birthstone Card Backs

Birthstone Card

January

garnet

Garnets range in color from green or red to black or colorless. A deep red is the most common color. Some ancient warriors wore garnets on their breastplates.

Birthstone Card

February

amethyst

Amethysts are purple quartz crystals. Amethysts can be found in many royal jewel collections, including the British Crown Jewels.

Birthstone Card

March

aquamarine

Aquamarines range between blue and blue-green. Aquamarines have been associated with the sea because of their blue color.

Birthstone Card

April

diamond

People usually think of diamonds as colorless. However, they can also be yellow, black, or even blue. Diamond is the hardest mineral in the world.

Birthstone Card

May

emerald

Emeralds come in many shades of green, and the name *emerald* comes from a Greek word meaning "green stone." Ancient Romans dedicated the emerald to their goddess Venus.

Birthstone Card

June

pearl

Pearls are usually white. However, they can be yellow, lavender, black, gray, purple, or blue as well. Pearls are not minerals. They form inside oysters and clams.

How the Earth Works, ©2002. Published by Chicago Review Press, Inc., 800-888-7471.

Birthstone Card Backs

Birthstone Card

July

ruby

Rubies are red. Their name comes from the Latin word *ruber*, meaning "red." Rubies are very rare and beautiful. Like emeralds, they are found decorating many royal objects.

Birthstone Card

August

peridot (pair-i-doe)
Peridots are usually green. However, they can be yellowish-brown or red as well. Ancient people called them *chrysolithos*, which means "golden stone." Peridots are one of the oldest known gemstones.

Birthstone Card

September

sapphire

Sapphires are usually blue. However, they can be pale pink, gray, colorless, green, violet, brown, or yellow as well as orange. Sapphire gets its name from an island in the Arabian Sea, Sappherine, where many sapphires were found in ancient times.

Birthstone Card

October

opal

Opals are made up of the colors of the rainbow. They can be green, blue, red, milky, and black. The Latin word *opalus* means "precious stone." The opal is a very soft and fragile gemstone.

Birthstone Card

November

topaz

Topaz can be green, yellow, pink, red, brown, or black. The word *topaz* means "fire" in Sanskrit. The crown jewels of Portugal include a famous yellow topaz.

Birthstone Card

December

turquoise

Turquoise is usually blue or blue-green. It is one of the earliest gemstones found in jewelry. It adorns objects and jewelry in ancient Egyptian tombs. Native Americans have been decorating jewelry with turquoise for thousands of years.

Earthquakes and Volcanoes

Earth's Power

Mt. St. Helens blew her top—
A 1980 show!
In her wake she left a mess,
A pyroclastic flow!
With trees flattened here,
Mud flowing there,
Here ashes!
There ashes!
Everywhere you turned—ASHES!
Mt. St. Helens blew her top—
Earth's power she did show.

Northridge really got a jolt
In '94 it's told.
In its wake it left a mess
Of buildings it did fold.
Bridges toppled here,
Freeways broken there,
Here a shake!
There a shake!
Everywhere the Earth quaked!
Northridge really got a jolt—
Earth's power it did show.

Sung to "Old MacDonald Had a Farm"
Rocks and Shocks: Singable Science Songs, ©2001

In Earthquakes and Volcanoes you will find

Wonderful Words from Earthquakes and Volcanoes

Active Volcano

This volcano is actually erupting or could erupt at any time.

Aftershocks

These smaller earthquakes occur after the main earthquake is over.

Caldera

This is the large, steep-walled crater left after a volcanic eruption.

Central Vent

The central chimneylike passageway that magma travels up through to Earth's surface during a volcanic eruption is called the central vent.

Continental Plates

These are the sections of Earth's crust that lie under the continents.

Dormant Volcano

This volcano is not erupting now and doesn't look like it will erupt any time soon, but it has erupted in the past and could could erupt again in the future.

Earthquake

Pressure under Earth's crust builds up until its plates snap and move, releasing stored energy. An earthquake is a sudden movement of Earth's crust caused by a release of energy stored in rocks.

Epicenter

A place on Earth's crust that is the center of the earthquake. It is above the earthquake's starting point, or focus. The earthquake is felt most strongly at the epicenter.

Extinct Volcano

A volcano that scientists predict will not erupt again is called an extinct volcano.

Friction

Friction occurs when two surfaces rub against each other.

Lapilli

These are very small stones propelled out of volcanoes during an eruption.

Lava

Once magma erupts out of Earth, it is called lava.

Lava Bombs

These are huge pieces of lava thrown out of volcanoes. They can be as large as houses.

Magma

Magma is the hot liquid rock below Earth's crust.

Magma Chamber

This is a chamber, or hollow place, in Earth's crust that fills to bursting with magma from beneath the crust, putting the magma under very high pressure.

Molten

Molten means "melted by heat."

Oceanic Plates

These gigantic pieces of Earth's crust lie under the oceans.

Pyroclastic Flow

This is a cloud of hot gas, ash, and lava debris that is blown out of a volcano during an eruption.

Richter Scale

The Richter scale measures the energy released, or magnitude, of an earthquake.

Seismic

This word comes from the Greek word meaning "shaking."

Seismologist

This is a scientist who studies earthquakes.

Subduction Zone

This is an area where one plate in Earth's crust dives beneath another plate.

Volcano

When the pressure in a magma chamber grows too great, ash, hot gases, and magma ooze or burst through a vent to Earth's surface, creating a volcano.

Volcanologist

This scientist studies volcanoes.

Dynamic Earth

What should I know about earthquakes and volcanoes?

🌐 Earth's plates are constantly moving. Most volcanoes and earthquakes happen along the edges of plates, where the plates meet. As plates slide by each other, they cause friction. The grinding of two sliding plates causes stress in the rocks below. This can result in an earthquake. Sometimes plates collide, forming mountain ranges. Most volcanoes are formed when two plates either collide or move apart. When oceanic plates separate, molten magma erupts and forms new crust under the ocean. The island Surtsey was formed during a volcanic explosion under the Icelandic Sea in 1963.

🌐 Vulcan was the name of the blacksmith of the Roman gods. A small island in the Mediterranean Sea is called *Vulcano*. Thousands of years ago, people living near the island believed that the fire, hot lava, and ash erupting from Vulcano came from Vulcan's forge. They imagined that the eruptions were caused by the work he was doing for their gods. This is how the word *volcano* originated.

🌐 Volcanologists are scientists who study volcanoes. A volcano can occur when intense pressure from magma and gases builds up under Earth's crust. A volcanic explosion sends ash, hot gases, and molten magma up through a crack, or vent, in the crust. Magma becomes lava when it comes out of Earth. Volcanoes can blow out very small stones called lapilli or huge lava bombs the size of a house. They can shoot boiling lava fountains 300 feet into the air. Lava can slowly ooze out of a volcano or lava rivers can flow at speeds of up to 30 miles per hour.

🌐 Erupting volcanoes are called active volcanoes. Sleeping, or dormant, volcanoes could erupt again. Extinct volcanoes are those that scientists believe will not erupt again—but sometimes the scientists are wrong.

🌐 Pompeii, a small village in Italy, was buried under volcanic ash in A.D. 79 when the volcano Mt. Vesuvius erupted. Approximately 2,000 people lost their lives. A fisherman rediscovered Pompeii in 1711.

🌀 Thousands of earthquakes take place on Earth every year. However, only 20 to 30 of them are large. The power of an earthquake is measured using the Richter scale.

There are stations positioned all over the world to measure Earth's movements.

🌀 People have been trying to predict earthquakes for centuries. Animals have been observed behaving strangely before an earthquake. Sometimes bodies of water have a peculiar smell before earthquakes. To date, no one has found an accurate way to predict earthquakes.

1 Best Guess—Volcano Trivia Cards

Did you know?
Volcanology is the scientific study of volcanoes.

You will need
Volcano Trivia Card Fronts, page 157, and Backs, page 158, copied onto 2 sheets of light-colored card stock (8½ × 11 inches)

Scissors

Glue

Partner

Rubber band

What do you think?
If I try to guess the answers for the Volcano Trivia questions, I will guess ___ out of 4 correctly.

Now you are ready to
1. Cut out the 16 Volcano Trivia cards.
2. Match the card fronts to their answer backs. Glue the matching card pieces together, back-to-back.
3. Place the cards with the question side up.
4. Ask your partner to give a best-guess answer to the first four questions. Check the backs of the cards to see if each question was answered correctly.
5. Next, it is your turn to guess the answers to the last four questions. How well did you guess?
6. Use the rubber band to keep the cards together.

 Activity Goal

To learn new information about volcanoes.

 Earth Note

Volcanologists wear special suits that protect them.

 Key to Success

Some children may need help cutting out and gluing the cards.

 Hint

Trivia cards are a fun way to learn new information.

Volcanoes Trivia Card Fronts

Volcanoes Trivia

What shoots out gases, hot molten lava, ash, and rock pieces from deep inside Earth?

Volcanoes Trivia

What happened to the 2,000 people who lived in Pompeii, Italy, in A.D. 79?

Volcanoes Trivia

Mt. St. Helens's 1980 eruption spread volcanic ash as far away as Minnesota and was as powerful as how many atomic bombs?

Volcanoes Trivia

Volcanoes have shot fountains of fire as high up as how many feet?

Volcanoes Trivia

What are scientists who study volcanoes called?

Volcanoes Trivia

Erupting volcanoes are called _____.

Volcanoes Trivia

Volcanoes are found on what other planets?

Volcanoes Trivia

Volcanoes that might erupt are called _____.

How the Earth Works, ©2002. Published by Chicago Review Press, Inc., 800-888-7471.

Volcanoes Trivia Card Backs

Volcanoes Trivia Answer ①	Volcanoes Trivia Answer ②
 volcanoes	Mt. Vesuvius erupted and the people of Pompeii were buried in 20 feet of ash.

Volcanoes Trivia Answer ③	Volcanoes Trivia Answer ④
500 atomic bombs	300 feet

Volcanoes Trivia Answer ⑤	Volcanoes Trivia Answer ⑥
volcanologists	active volcanoes

Volcanoes Trivia Answer ⑦	Volcanoes Trivia Answer ⑧
Mars, Jupiter, and Venus	dormant volcanoes

How the Earth Works, ©2002. Published by Chicago Review Press, Inc., 800-888-7471.

2 Earthquake Fact or Fiction

Did you know?
The 1994 Northridge earthquake, near Los Angeles, California, was a very powerful earthquake.

You will need
Earthquake Fact or Fiction Card Fronts, page 160, and Backs, page 161, copied onto 2 sheets of light-colored card stock

Scissors

Glue

Partner

Rubber band

What do you think?
If I try to guess the answers for Earthquake Fact or Fiction, I will guess __ out of 4 correctly.

Now you are ready to
1. Cut out the 16 Earthquake Fact or Fiction cards.
2. Match the card fronts to their answer backs. Glue the matching card pieces together, back-to-back.
3. Place the cards with the answer side down.
4. Ask your partner to guess fact or fiction to the first four cards. Each time, check the back of the card to see if he or she was right.
5. Next, it is your turn to guess fact or fiction for the last four cards. How well did you guess?

 Activity Goal
To learn new information about earthquakes in a fun fact or fiction card game.

 Earth Note
The 1995 earthquake in Kobe, Japan, twisted train tracks and ruined 2,000 feet of highway.

 Key to Success
Some children may need help cutting out and gluing the cards.

 Hint
These cards are a great way for children to learn new information.

Earthquake Fact or Fiction Card Fronts

Earthquake Fact or Fiction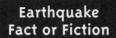

The longest recorded earthquake lasted 4 minutes.

Earthquake Fact or Fiction

There are hundreds of earthquakes every year.

Earthquake Fact or Fiction

Some animals behave strangely before earthquakes.

Earthquake Fact or Fiction

A pyramid-shaped building is not very sturdy in an earthquake.

Earthquake Fact or Fiction

A moonquake occurs on the moon.

Earthquake Fact or Fiction

It is important to duck and cover in an earthquake.

Earthquake Fact or Fiction

A creepmeter is a machine used to measure Earth's plate movements.

Earthquake Fact or Fiction

The Richter scale measures the power of an earthquake.

Earthquake Fact or Fiction Card Backs

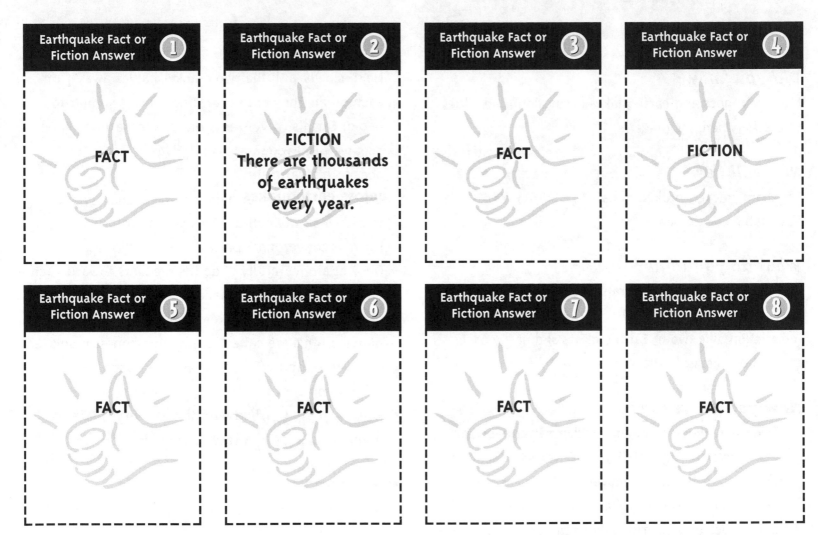

Earthquake Fact or Fiction Answer ① FACT	**Earthquake Fact or Fiction Answer** ② FICTION There are thousands of earthquakes every year.	**Earthquake Fact or Fiction Answer** ③ FACT	**Earthquake Fact or Fiction Answer** ④ FICTION
Earthquake Fact or Fiction Answer ⑤ FACT	**Earthquake Fact or Fiction Answer** ⑥ FACT	**Earthquake Fact or Fiction Answer** ⑦ FACT	**Earthquake Fact or Fiction Answer** ⑧ FACT

3 Plate Movements

Did you know?

Most volcanoes and earthquakes occur along the edges of plates, where they meet.

You will need

1 graham cracker, broken in half
Resealable plastic bag

What do you think?

If I slide the edges of two graham crackers past each other, they (will) or (won't) rub against each other, causing friction, like two of Earth's plates sliding by each other and causing friction.

Now you are ready to

1. Slowly slide the two graham cracker halves past each other with their edges sliding against each other in opposite directions. This movement is similar to Earth's plates sliding past each other. Where Earth's plates rub against each other, earthquakes can happen.

2. Next, slowly pull the two cracker halves away from each other. They are separating. This is similar to two of Earth's (divergent) plates separating. When oceanic plates separate, underwater volcanoes can occur.

3. Move the two cracker halves toward each other so that they slowly collide. This is similar to two of Earth's (convergent) plates slowly colliding.

4. Once again, carefully slide the crackers toward each other until they meet. Make the right cracker slowly dive under the left cracker. Areas where Earth's plates do this are called subduction zones. Increased earthquake and volcanic activity occurs in subduction zones.

5. When you are finished with this activity, place the graham crackers in a resealable plastic bag.

Brain exercise

When I made one of the crackers dive, I thought . . .

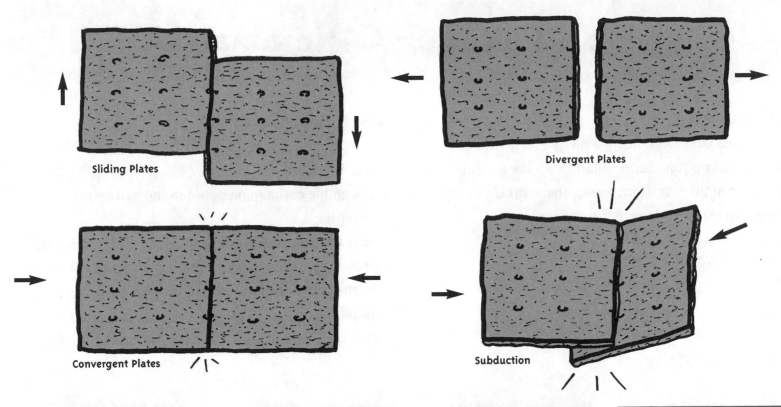

Sliding Plates

Divergent Plates

Convergent Plates

Subduction

🏆 **Activity Goal**	🌍 **Earth Note**	👍 **Key to Success**	⭐ **Hint**
To demonstrate four types of plate movements.	Volcanoes and earthquakes provide information about Earth's temperature, pressure, and structure.	Use fresh, crisp graham crackers. Each child should have his or her own crackers.	If the children use too much pressure, the crackers will break. Eating the crackers after this activity is a fun reward.

4 Inside a Volcano—A Triorama

Did you know?

The magma chamber holds the molten magma that has traveled up from Earth's mantle. As the pressure from heat in the mantle increases, the magma pushes its way up through vents to the surface.

You will need

Triorama Design, page 165, copied onto white paper

Scissors

Colored pencils (optional)

Paste or glue stick

Now you are ready to

1. Cut out the Triorama Design. Color in the volcano if you like.
2. Cut on the cutting line between the two empty triangles.
3. Fold the large volcano triangle up at the fold line.
4. Fold the smaller "My Volcano" triangle over the top of the empty triangle. Paste the two triangles together.
5. Display your volcano triorama in a special place.

Activity Goal	Earth Note	Key to Success	Hint
To identify the basic parts of a volcano.	The main chimneylike structure in a volcano is called the central vent.	Discuss the parts of the volcano with the children. See Wonderful Words, p. 152.	To learn about volcanoes from the experts, visit the Web sites listed on page 183.

Triorama Design

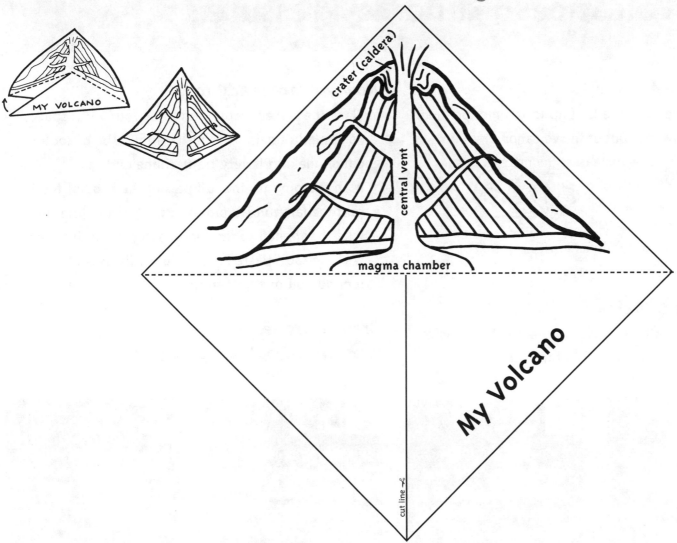

crater (caldera)

central vent

magma chamber

My Volcano

MY VOLCANO

cut line

5 Volcanoes—Building Pressure

Did you know?

Lava rivers can flow at speeds of up to 30 miles per hour or lava can slowly ooze out of the volcano.

You will need

Adult helper
Waxed paper
1 sample-sized tube of toothpaste with cap on
1 pushpin

What do you think?

If I make a hole in a tube of toothpaste, the toothpaste (will) or (won't) slowly ooze out of the tube.

Now you are ready to

1. Place the waxed paper on top of your work space.
2. Ask an adult helper to push on the tube of toothpaste, making it very tight at one end.
3. Push the pin into the full part of the tube of toothpaste. Then quickly pull it out.
4. What happened to the toothpaste? What did it do? Was the toothpaste under a lot of pressure? Did it remind you of a volcano?

Brain exercise

When I saw the toothpaste come out, I thought . . .

Activity Goal	Earth Note	Key to Success	Hint
To compare the oozing toothpaste to the slow ooze of a Hawaiian eruption.	Some volcanic eruptions ooze out lava and produce large but low volcanoes. These are called *Hawaiian eruptions.*	Put enough pressure on the toothpaste tube to make toothpaste flow out of the hole. Use a new tube.	This is a fun activity. Use duct tape to cover the hole after the activity is completed.

6 Volcanoes—Flowing Fountain

Did you know?

Volcanoes can blow out very small stones called lapilli or huge lava bombs. Some volcanoes shoot boiling lava fountains 300 feet into the air.

You will need

Adult helper wearing an apron

Outdoor area

1 can strawberry pop

1 tall (21 ounces) clear plastic container with lid

Pushpin

What do you think?

If I shake up a can of pop and then poke a hole in it, the pop (will) or (won't) slowly ooze out of the can.

Now you are ready to

1. In an outdoor area, carefully shake the can of pop to increase the amount of pressure inside.
2. Stand the pop can inside the plastic container.
3. Ask an adult to use the pushpin to poke a hole in the can's lid and then quickly pull his or her hand out of the container and put on the container lid.
4. Watch the pop come out of the can. Why does it do that? What does it look like to you?

Brain exercise

When the pin was stuck in the can, I thought . . .

Activity Goal

To demonstrate a release of built-up pressure.

Earth Note

Vulcanian eruptions shoot out thick lava and lava bombs. Plinian eruptions shoot gas, ash, and cinders great distances.

Key to Success

For best results, shake the can immediately before it is punctured.

Hint

Shake a bottle of root beer and then loosen the top to see a more flowing release of pressure.

7 Erupting Volcano

Did you know?

In a Peléean eruption, thick, sticky lava oozes down the volcano sides and is then followed by a cloud of ash and gas.

You will need

Scissors

Small cone-shaped coffee filter

Plastic container lid large enough to protect the floor under a baby food jar

1/2 cup baking soda in a small baby food jar

1/2 cup vinegar containing 1 drop red food coloring

What do you think?

If I pour red vinegar into a jar of baking soda, it (will) or (won't) erupt like a volcano.

Now you are ready to

1. Put the plastic container lid under the baby food jar.
2. Cut off the pointed end of the coffee filter and slip it over the outside of the open baby food jar.
3. Slowly pour the red vinegar onto the baking soda inside the jar.
4. What happens? Does it remind you of an erupting volcano?

Brain exercise

When I poured the vinegar onto the baking soda, it . . .

 Activity Goal

To simulate a volcanic eruption.

 Earth Note

Mt. St. Helens's 1980 eruption was as powerful as 500 atomic bombs going off.

 Key to Success

Make sure to protect all clothing. The red food coloring stains.

Hint

The children love this activity. It's a great activity to do outside on a sunny day.

8 Take a Closer Look—Volcanic Froth

Did you know?

Pumice is a form of hardened lava. Pumice is called *volcanic froth* because it is full of air bubbles and very light in weight.

You will need

Specimen 15, pumice stone, from Rocks and Minerals Collection Starter, activivty #2, page 86.

Plastic container of water

Rocks and Minerals case

What do you think?

If I place a pumice stone in water, it (will) or (won't) sink.

Now you are ready to

1. Place the pumice stone in the container of water.
2. Does the pumice stone sink or float? Is this what you predicted it would do? Why do you think the pumice floated?
3. Let the pumice stone sit in the water for an hour. What happens after an hour? Why do you think this happens?
4. What are the special properties of pumice?
5. Place the pumice back in your collection case.

Brain Exercise

When I saw all of the holes in the pumice, I thought . . .

 Activity Goals

To observe pumice in water. To identify the properties of pumice.

 Earth Note

The density of pumice is so low that it can float.

 Key to Success

Discuss how pumice is formed and how it eventually sinks as the holes fill with water.

 Hint

Ask the children to predict how long it will take for the pumice to sink.

9 Pressure and Release

Did you know?

Energy is the power to move or change things. Pressure under Earth's crust builds up until the plates snap and move to release built-up energy. An earthquake is a sudden movement of Earth's crust caused by a release of energy stored in rocks.

You will need

1 piece uncooked spaghetti
1 graham cracker
1 craft stick

Now you are ready to

1. Pick up the piece of uncooked spaghetti. Watch and listen as you snap it in half. Did it make a very loud sound? Was it hard to break? Did it bend before it broke? Do you think that it released much energy when it broke? The snap happened when the pressure you put on the piece of spaghetti became stronger than the spaghetti itself. The release of energy when it snapped is similar to the release of energy stored in rocks when an earthquake occurs.

2. Next, watch and listen to the sound made as you snap the graham cracker in half. Did it make a very loud sound? Was it as hard or harder to break than the piece of spaghetti? Was more energy released when it broke than when the piece of spaghetti broke?

3. Try to break the craft stick in half. Watch and listen as you break it. How loud was the sound that it made? Was it as hard or harder to break than the piece of spaghetti and the graham cracker? Was more energy released when it broke than when the piece of spaghetti or the cracker broke?

Brain Exercise

When I watched the craft stick bend until it snapped, I thought . . .

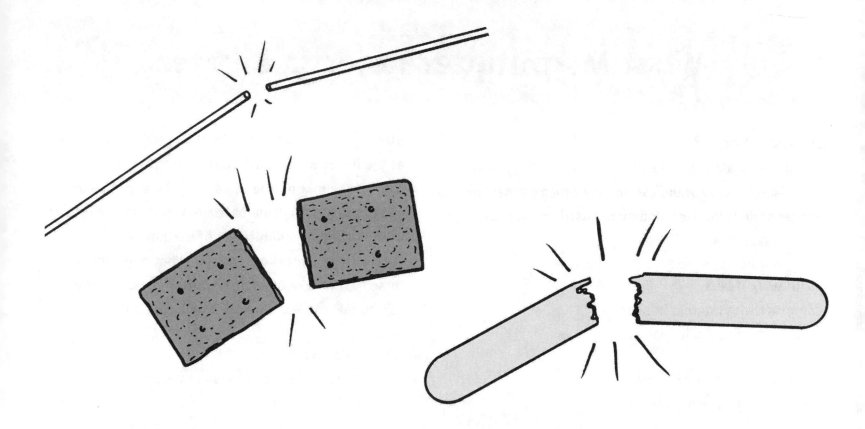

Activity Goal

To observe a gradual buildup of pressure and then release of energy.

Earth Note

The more built-up pressure, the larger the earthquake will be.

Key to Success

The activity needs to be done in a quiet area. Each child should have his or her own materials.

Hint

Crackers must be very fresh. Once the activity is finished, children enjoy eating their crackers.

10   What Magnitude? Refer to Richter

Did you know?

The Richter scale measures the amount of energy released by an earthquake, or the earthquake's magnitude. The Richter scale is the most commonly used measure of an earthquake's power.

You will need

Computer with Internet hookup
Modified Richter Scale, page 173

Now you are ready to

1. Go to the Internet Web site http://quake.wr.usgs.gov/more/eqfaq.html to look at the list of major earthquakes worldwide.
2. Look at the magnitude of each of the earthquakes.
3. Check the Richter scale on page 173 to see the effects of the different magnitudes of earthquakes.
4. Look at the Richter scale again. What might happen in an earthquake of each magnitude? How many earthquakes of each magnitude happen per year?

Brain exercise

When I looked at the Richter scale, I thought . . .

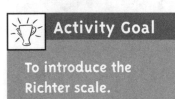 **Activity Goal**

To introduce the Richter scale.

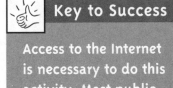 **Earth Note**

The more energy released, the higher the magnitude of the earthquake.

 Key to Success

Access to the Internet is necessary to do this activity. Most public libraries have Internet.

Hint

Check out the other exciting Web sites listed on page 183.

Modified Richter Scale

Magnitude 1–2	Magnitude 2–3	Magnitude 3–4	Magnitude 4–5

Only detected by instruments such as seismographs. (Over half a million per year.)	Detected by instruments and only felt a little by people. (Hundreds of thousands per year.)	Felt slightly. Bells might ring, lights might move. (Tens of thousands per year.)	Felt strongly. Some glass and building damage occurs. (Thousands per year.)
2.0 = 13 lbs TNT	3.0 = 397 lbs TNT	4.0 = 6 tons TNT	5.0 = 199 tons TNT

Magnitude 5–6	Magnitude 6–7	Magnitude 7–8	Magnitude 8–9
		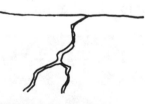	
Felt strongly. There is building damage. (Hundreds per year.)	Severe. Buildings and chimneys collapse. (Twenty to 200 per year.)	Severe. Buildings collapse and cracks form in the ground. (Ten to 20 per year.)	Mass destruction. Buildings, bridges, and roads collapse. (Ten or fewer per year.)
6.0 = 6,270 tons TNT	7.0 = 199,000 tons TNT	8.0 = 6,270,000 tons TNT	9.0 = 199,999,000 tons TNT

How the Earth Works, ©2002. Published by Chicago Review Press, Inc., 800-888-7471.

11   Waves of Motion I—Color Ripples

Did you know?

The energy released by an earthquake travels through the ground in the form of waves. Shock waves start deep underground when rocks release stored-up energy. This starting point is called the focus of an earthquake.

You will need

Large bowl of water
1 drop of dark food coloring

What do you think?

If I place a drop of food coloring into a bowl of water, I (will) or (won't) be able to see waves spreading out from the drop.

Now you are ready to

1. Observe the water. What does it look like?
2. Place 1 drop of food coloring into the center of the water.
3. What do you see? Does the water ripple around the drop? Why do you think it is rippling?

Brain exercise

When I saw the food coloring rippling through the water, I thought . . .

 Activity Goal

To create and observe the rippling effect caused by vibrations.

 Earth Note

Earthquake vibrations move outward in all directions from the starting point, or focus. The epicenter is the place on Earth's crust that is above the focus.

 Key to Success

Only use 1 drop of food coloring. The darker the color, the better the effect.

 Hint

To reinforce this concept, talk about the effect of throwing a stone into a lake.

12 Waves of Motion II—Rippling Rope

Did you know?

An earthquake is a sudden release of stored energy. This release makes some of Earth's plates slip and shake. Waves of energy travel up to the surface crust.

You will need

Long rope
Partner

What do you think?

The harder I shake the rope, the (more) or (less) energy will be released.

Now you are ready to

1. Place the rope flat on the ground.
2. Keeping the rope on the ground, you and your partner should each hold one end of the rope.
3. Ask your partner to gently shake the rope up and down while you keep your end flat on the ground.

Watch the motion of the rope. What did you observe? Did you see waves? Where were the waves the largest? Why?

4. Ask your partner to shake the rope a bit harder as you keep your end flat on the ground. Again, watch the motion of the rope. How is this motion different than the last? Why do you think it changed?
5. Ask your partner to give the rope a hard shake. How did the waves change?
6. Next, you can shake the rope as your partner keeps his or her end flat.

Brain exercise

When I shook the rope hard, I saw . . .

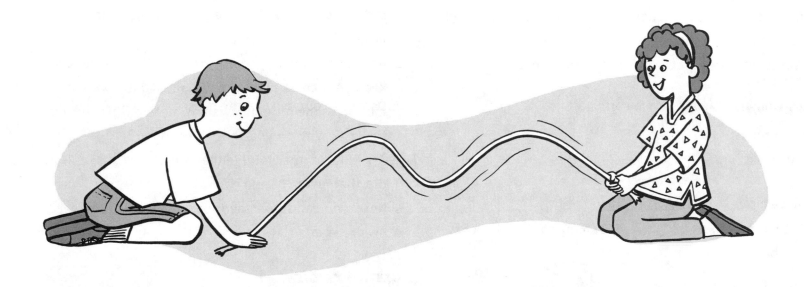

 Activity Goal

To demonstrate how the size of a wave decreases as it moves away from its energy source.

 Earth Note

Aftershocks are smaller earthquakes that happen after the larger earthquake.

 Key to Success

Make sure the rope stays on the ground during this activity.

 Hint

Tie this activity into activity #11.

13 Solid Foundations?

Did you know?

The type of ground under a house affects what will happen to it in an earthquake.

You will need

2 small, clean, empty milk cartons

Decorating supplies

1 aluminum container (small cake pan) filled with dry sand

1 aluminum container (small cake pan) filled with wet sand

Metal table or desk

What do you think?

If my milk-carton house is standing on wet sand, it (will) or (won't) sink more than if it is standing on dry sand.

Now you are ready to

1. Decorate your milk-carton houses.
2. Place a milk-carton house in each of the sand containers.
3. Place the aluminum sand containers on the table.
4. Bang your fist on the table between the two containers. What happens to your houses?
5. Why do you think the houses react the way they do?

Brain exercise

When the house is standing on dry sand, it . . .

 Activity Goal

To compare how two different types of soil affect the stability of structures in an earthquake.

 Earth Note

When buildings are built on wet soil, they are much more likely to be damaged by an earthquake.

 Key to Success

The milk-carton houses must be the same size. The small cartons used for school lunches work well.

 Hint

Check the wet sand before the activity to make sure it hasn't dried out.

14 Shake-a-Quake!

Did you know?

The way a building is designed affects how well it can handle an earthquake.

You will need

Plastic container holding a 3- to 4-inch square of Jell-O Jiggler

Bag of miniature marshmallows (colored are fun)

1 box round toothpicks

Now you are ready to

1. Using the marshmallows, construct a structure on the Jell-O Jiggler square.

2. Once you are finished building the structure, gently shake your container of Jell-O. What happens to your structure when the Jell-O ground shakes?

3. Think about what might help your marshmallow building stay standing during an earthquake.

4. Using the toothpicks and marshmallows, design a structure that stands up better in an earthquake. Test each structure by gently shaking the container to make an earthquake.

5. What did you learn about building structures and earthquakes?

Activity Goals	**Earth Note**	**Key to Success**	**Hint**
To demonstrate how building materials affect stability in an earthquake. To evaluate a structure's design.	Today's buildings use steel rods (rebar) to make them more stable in an earthquake.	Jell-O Jigglers work well because they are so firm.	If you are working with a group of children, use a paper plate with a 3-inch square Jell-O Jiggler on it per child.

Chapter-by-Chapter Content and Skills Guide

Content Area

Content Area	1	2	3	4	5
Building materials					•
Cast fossils		•			
Chemical reactions			•		
Contents	•				
Crystals				•	
Crystal growing				•	
Crystal products				•	
Dinosaurs		•			
Earth structure	•				
Earthquakes					•
Energy					•
Equator	•				
Fossils		•			
Fossil fuels		•			
Gaseous state	•	•		•	
Gems				•	
Gemstones				•	
Glaciers		•			
Igneous rock			•		
Liquid state	•	•	•		
Magnetism			•		
Metamorphic rock			•	•	
Minerals			•	•	
Mohs' Scale of Hardness			•		
Mold fossils		•			
Mountain type	•				
Paleontology		•			

Content Area (cont.)	1	2	3	4	5
Pangaea	•				
Physical properties		•	•		•
Pressure					•
Richter scale					•
Rocks			•		
Safety issues					•
Sedimentary rock			•		
Seismology					•
Soil					•
Solid state	•	•	•		
Streak test			•		
Technology					•
Trace fossils		•			
Vibrations					•
Volcanoes					•
Zone fossils		•			

Science Skill

Science Skill	1	2	3	4	5
Classifying		•	•	•	•
Collaborating	•	•	•	•	
Collecting	•				
Communicating	•	•	•	•	
Comparing	•				•
Constructing	•			•	•
Contrasting	•				•
Demonstrating	•	•		•	•
Designing					•
Evaluating	•	•	•		•

Examining	•	•	•	•	•
Identifying	•	•	•	•	•
Investigating	•	•	•	•	•
Matching	•	•	•	•	•
Measuring	•	•	•	•	•
Modeling	•	•	•	•	•
Observing	•	•	•	•	•
Planning	•	•	•	•	•
Predicting	•	•	•	•	•
Problem solving	•	•	•	•	•
Recording	•	•	•	•	•
Researching				•	•
Simulating	•				•
Testing	•				•

Across the Curriculum

Across the Curriculum	1	2	3	4	5
Art	•	•	•	•	•
Cooking	•	•			
Geography	•	•	•		•
Health				•	
History	•	•	•		•
Language Arts	•	•	•		•
Mathematics	•	•	•	•	
Music	•	•			
Safety			•	•	
Social Studies	•	•			•

Answer Sheets

Chapter 1 How Earth Is Put Together

What's That Continent? Bingo Board

1 Africa
2 Pangaea
3 Asia
4 Australia

6 South America
7 North America
8 Europe
9 Antarctica

Chapter 2 Fantastic Fossils

Name That Fossil! Bingo Board

1 ancient shark tooth
2 amber
3 ammonite
4 fossil snail
7 trilobite
8 belemnite
9 dinosaur eggshell fragment

Chapter 3 Revealing Rocks and Minerals

Mineral Identification I—Scratch It!

Specimen 1 is calcite.
Specimen 3 is talcum.
Specimen 4 is apatite.

Name That Rock! Bingo Board

limestone	sedimentary
shale	sedimentary
granite	igneous
slate	metamorphic
sandstone	sedimentary
pumice	igneous
obsidian	igneous
talcum	metamorphic
marble	metamorphic

Product and Service Information

Rocks and Shocks: Singable Science Songs CD
©2001 by Michelle O'Brien-Palmer and Nancy Stewart
MicNik Publications, Inc. & Friends Street Music
ISBN # 1-885430-22-1, UPC 79188201142
6505 SE 28th, Mercer Island, WA 98040
(206) 232-1078, micnik@aol.com, http://www.micnik.com

Specimen Sets for Fossils, Minerals, Rocks, and Crystals

Rockman McLean Trading Company
PO Box 7174
Loveland, CO 80537
(970) 622-0869; rocksandminerals.com/menu.htm
(Mention that you are buying these items for the *Rocks and Shocks* book activities)

Jerry's Rocks and Gems
804 West Valley Highway
Kent, WA 98032
(253) 852-0539
jerrysrockandgem@msn.com, http://www.jerrysrockandgem.com

Earth Science Services for Elementary Schools

School Assemblies and Workshops
Dynamic Earth Interactive School Assemblies
Presenters: Michelle O'Brien-Palmer and Nancy Stewart
12533 197th CT NE, Woodinville, WA 98072
(425) 881-6476, micnik@aol.com, http://www.micnik.com

Classroom Workshops

Presenter: Bob Jackson, Geology Adventures
P.O. Box 809, Ravensdale, WA 98051
(425) 413-1122, geologyadventur@seanet.com
http://www.geologyadventures.com/

Learn More About It!

Books and Internet Resources

Books

Melvin Berger and Gilda Berger
Why Do Volcanoes Blow?
Scholastic, 1999

Ann-Jeanette Campbell and Ronald Rood
Incredible Earth: A Book of Answers for Kids
Michael Friedman Publishing Company, Inc., 1991

Carol Carrick
Patrick's Dinosaurs
Clarion, 1983

Neil Curtis and Michael Allaby
Planet Earth
Kingfisher Books, 1993

Cally Hall
Gem Stones
Dorling Kindersley, Inc., 1994

Rupert Hochleitner
Minerals: Identifying,Classifying, and Collecting Them
Barron's Education Series, Inc., 1994

Martin Holden
The Encyclopedia of Gemstones and Minerals
Michael Friedman Publishing Company, Inc., 1991

Eldridge Moores
Volcanoes & Earthquakes
Time-Life Books, 1995

Chris Pellant
The Complete Book of Rocks and Minerals
DK Publishing Book, 1995

Chris Pellant
Fossils
Thunder Bay Press, 1994

Paul Taylor
Fossils
Knopf, 1990

Herbert Zim and Paul Shaffer
Rocks and Minerals: A Guide to Familiar Minerals, Gems, Ores, and Rocks
Golden Press, 1954

Internet Web Sites

Continental Drift
http://kids.mtpe.hq.nasa.gov/archive/pangea/evidence.html
NASA

http://duke.usask.ca/~reeves/prog/geoe118/geoe118.057.html
Department of Geological Sciences, University of Saskatchewan

Earth
http://earthsky.com
Earth & Sky

Faults and Stresses
http://duke.usask.ca/~reeves/prog/geoe118/geoe118.051.html
Department of Geological Sciences, University of Saskatchewan

http://duke.usask.ca/~reeves/prog/geoe118/geoe118.051.html
Department of Geological Sciences, University of Saskatchewan

Fossil Parks Around the Country
http://www.discovery.com/exp/fossilzone/map.html
Discovery.com

Join a Dig—Fossil Hunting Adventures
http://www.discovery.com/exp/fossilzone/map.html
Discovery.com

Plate Movement
http://library.thinkquest.org/17701/high/tectonics/index.html
Think Quest.org

The Rock Cycle
http://duke.usask.ca/~reeves/prog/geoe118/geoe118.011.html
Department of Geological Sciences, University of Saskatchewan

Volcanoes
http://www.learner.org/exhibits/volcanoes/resources.html
Annenberg/CPB Exhibits

Acknowledgments

Thanks to:

Eric Beam, for his unfaltering support of my work.

Tom Bleier, scientist, inventor, and lifelong learner, for inspiring children and adults through his quest to find a scientific method for earthquake prediction.

Eileen Gibbons, Earth science teacher and more, for inspiring me to write this book through her love of our dynamic Earth.

Joan Knudsen, paleontologist, for her consultation and rock cookie ideas.

George Leighton (Georgie the Geologist), geologist and friend, for his consultation on activity content.

Linda Matthews, publisher, Chicago Review Press, for her thorough editing.

Gid Palmer, for his wonderful support of my efforts on this project.

Nick Palmer, for listening patiently to poetry sung to childhood tunes at the dinner table, and worse.

Corinne Richardson, third-grade teacher, for her positive outlook in life and her inspiring love of our dynamic Earth.

Resort Semi-ah-moo staff, for their support during the idea generation and editing phases of this book.

Evelyn Sansky, for 35 years of friendship and her support of my creative adventures.

Jan Johnson Stollee, for her friendship and flexibility with regard to my projects.

Tom Yelin, USGS, University of Washington, for his consultation on various Earth facts and figures.

Thanks to the following Lake Washington School District teachers for their flexibility, suggestions, and opening up their classrooms to countless hours of activity testing. This book could not have been written without their support and the contributions of their eager young scientists: Mrs. Casey Crane, Mrs. LeeAnn Jackson, and Mrs. Corinne Richardson.

Student Contributors:
Mrs. Jackson's first-grade class
Braden Bouwman
Alison Cary
Stephanie Chi
Taycan Darling
Patrick Donohoe
James Gee
Andre Gomez
Hannah Graziadio
Nicole Guptil
Ali Hyder
Tian Kisch

James Over
Chris Pribbernow
Tristan Rawas
Victoria Ruryk
Chase Schmidt
Cori Shull
Franco Simone
Katie Staudinger
Tony Veintimilla
Emily Wolowski
Tessa Yip
Mrs. Richardson's third-grade class
Matthew Burbidge
Athena Burkholder
Katrina Carpenter
Blakeley Cathcart
Sean Cheng
Brooke Davis
Ashton Hemphill
Kylene Ingle
Jessa Link
Allen Liu
Colleen Lorentson
Kyle McDonnell
Caitlin McLuskie
Emily Mortenson
Kaylene Nadalin
Alan Nguyen
Michael Russo
Jonathon Shi
Sloane Smith
Jordan Thomas

David Uno
Brandon Zaffiro
Dylan Zeitllin
Mrs. Crane's second/third-grade class
Taylor Backous
Christopher Berg
Jena Boyle
Tyler Browne
Blake Cassidy
Christian Cook
Evan Goronkin
Emma Hannigan
Caitlin Hanson
Michelle Jackson
Daniel Jackstadt
Carolyn Kading
Elisabeth Kirsten
Megan Leierzapf
Arjun Malhotra
Jordan Moon
Nayah Nshom
Alexander Pett
Isabell Sakamoto
Maloné Shibley
Carlyle Skinner
Natalie Jean White